AF427493

Welcome To
CAPITOL TIMES MAGAZINE
GET YOUR SUBSCRIPTION
TODAY!

www.capitoltimesmedia.com/magazine-subscription

American Patriot Relief

American Patriot Relief is an all volunteer non-profit organization designed by J6ers to support all January 6 defendants and their family in these tumultuous times. While we do not provide legal fees, we do help with life's financial needs, whatever it might be. We provide help with travel to D.C. for the defendant and family. We also have the most robust and personalized commissary program for donors with our Adopt-a-J6er program. Additionally, we have the 833-SAVEDJ6 hotline for J6ers and their family. 833-SAVEDJ6 is a 24/7 hotline, staffed by volunteers ready to help with emotional and financial support. We also host a "meet-and-greet" Zoom call every Monday and a Tuesday "Payer Vigil" linking up with Freedom Corner in D.C. to pray for our J6 Hostages.
To get involved and help all J6ers scan the QR below or log on to americanpatriotrelief.org.
You can also find us on X (Twitter) and Telegram.
It's time we take a stand for those that stood for us.

Capitol Times
Magazine

www.capitoltimesmedia.com

Editor-In-Chief
Anil Anwar

Associate Editor
David Colbert

Magazine Graphic design
Capitol Times Graphic Team

Front Cover
Photo Source/Provided By:
Roger Stone

Photos
Canva.com
Trump White House - Flickr

Capitol Times Magazine

Owned by Capitol Times Media LLC
Printed in the United States of America
©All Rights Reserved - 2024

www.capitoltimesmedia.com
editor@capitoltimesmedia.com

Disclaimer

ATTENTION ADVERTISERS AND SPONSORS!

Capitol Times magazine is on the lookout for partners who share our commitment to truth and the promotion of Christian Conservative values. As a trusted publication in the United States, we strive to uphold the highest standards of journalism while championing principles that resonate with our readership.

By advertising with us, you not only gain access to our loyal audience but also align your brand with a publication that stands firm in its dedication to integrity and authenticity. Your support will enable us to continue delivering insightful content that informs, educates, and inspires.

Join us in our mission to make a difference in the world of media. Contact us today to explore advertising and sponsorship opportunities with Capitol Times magazine. Together, let's amplify the voice of conservatism and uphold the values that matter most.

Subscribe today to gain exclusive access to in-depth analysis, thought-provoking commentary, and expert opinions. Stay informed and engaged with the latest developments shaping our nation and world.

Subscribe now to Capitol Times Magazine and elevate your understanding of conservative principles and ideologies.

SUBSCRIBE TODAY AND GET STARTED!

www.capitoltimesmedia.com/magazine-subscription

Editor's Note

In this issue of Capitol Times Magazine, we are privileged to feature an exclusive interview with Roger Stone—a figure known for his unwavering dedication to American values and his steadfast faith in Christ Jesus.

Roger Stone's journey from personal to political advisor is nothing short of remarkable. He has navigated the intricacies of Washington politics with both conviction and courage, remaining a steadfast advocate for conservative principles and the ideals that have defined our nation.

In our conversation, Stone delves into his unique perspective on the Presidential elections, offering valuable insights shaped by decades of experience at the forefront of American politics. His views are both insightful and thought-provoking, reflecting a deep commitment to advancing the conservative cause.

As a true patriot and follower of Christ Jesus, Roger Stone embodies the values that Capitol Times Magazine seeks to uphold—integrity, resilience, and an unwavering dedication to the principles that have made America great.

We invite our readers to delve into this engaging interview, gaining a deeper understanding of Roger Stone's personal journey and his perspectives on the critical issues.

Roger Stone's story serves as a testament to the enduring spirit of those who strive to make a difference and uphold the timeless principles that define our great nation.

Anil Anwar

Editor-in-Chief
Capitol Times Magazine

Stay Informed with Capitol Times Magazine!

Your Ultimate Source for US National News, Right in the Heart of Capitol.
Grab Your Copy Today and Stay Ahead of the Times!

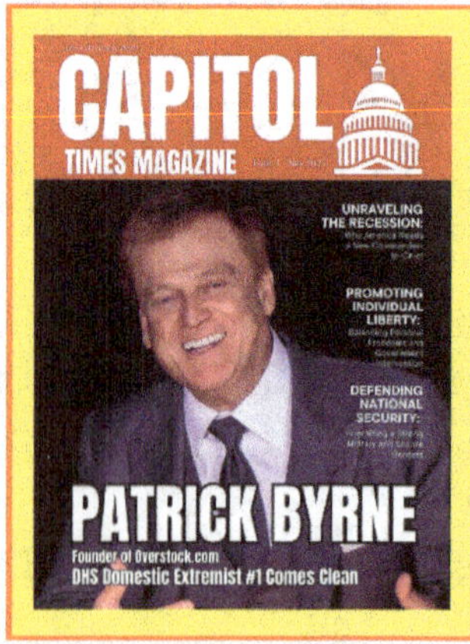

CAPITOL TIMES MAGAZINE

CONTENTS

ISSUE 09

APRIL | 2024

www.capitoltimesmedia.com

14 WHY ABORTION DECISIONS SHOULD REST WITH THE STATES
By Anil Anwar

40 THE NEW 2024 TRUMP BUS
Buddy Hall

42 MARK MIDDLETON
American Patriot Relief

19

HILLARY CLINTON'S 47
Disconnect with American Voters: A Lesson in Political Hubris
By David Colbert

THE HUNTER BIDEN SAGA: 51
Questionable Meetings and Congressional Defiance
By Mary Jones

54 THE UNFOLDING ELECTORAL LANDSCAPE:
A Christian Conservative Perspective
By Sunil Anwar

RELIGION SECTION

59 CHRISTIAN PERSECUTION IN ISLAMIC COUNTRIES:
A Call for Action and Support
By Pastor AS John

BUSINESS SECTION

66 HOW TO START A CONSERVATIVE BUSINESS:
A Practical Guide
By James Anderson

68 Rising Housing Costs Diminish Homeownership Dreams
By Mary Jones

Advertisement

Capitol Times Magazine Issue 8

Sponsored by

Budy Hall & American Patriot Relife

Review Rating

Thomas S

A must read. Turn off the TV. Sit down and read this. Then read it again.

Julie B

All Americans MUST read! This story is amazing and one every American must know.

Leslie D Keller

Important and great article on Patrick Byrne.
Everybody needs to read this.

Review Rating

Martha Boneta

Excellent Magazine featuring Patrick Byrne.
Exceptional journalism and cover story featuring Patrick Byrne!

★ ★ ★ ★ ★

David Colbert

A Riveting Read: Capitol Times Magazine Unveils the Truth about the Deep State

★ ★ ★ ★ ★

It reveals shocking details about our intelligence agencies, our election system, and how our intelligence community seeks successful and powerful resources from the private sector to help them achieve objectives. America is in peril from foreign enemies and we must peacefully unite if we want to save our country. Time is running short for us to be successful.

★ ★ ★ ★ ★

BROGUE
Signature
www.broguesignature.com

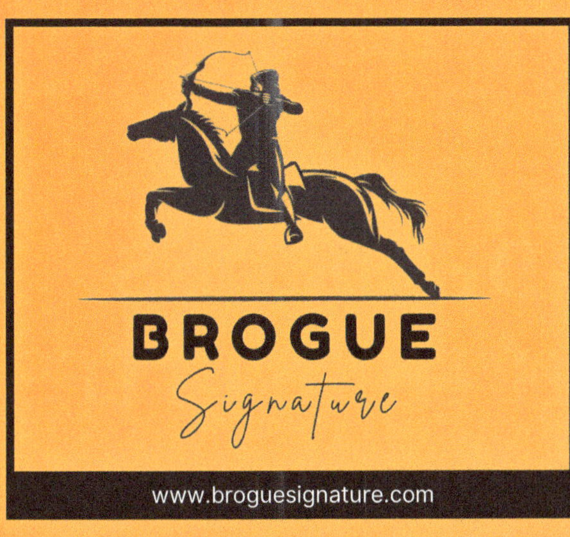

SUMMER FASHION

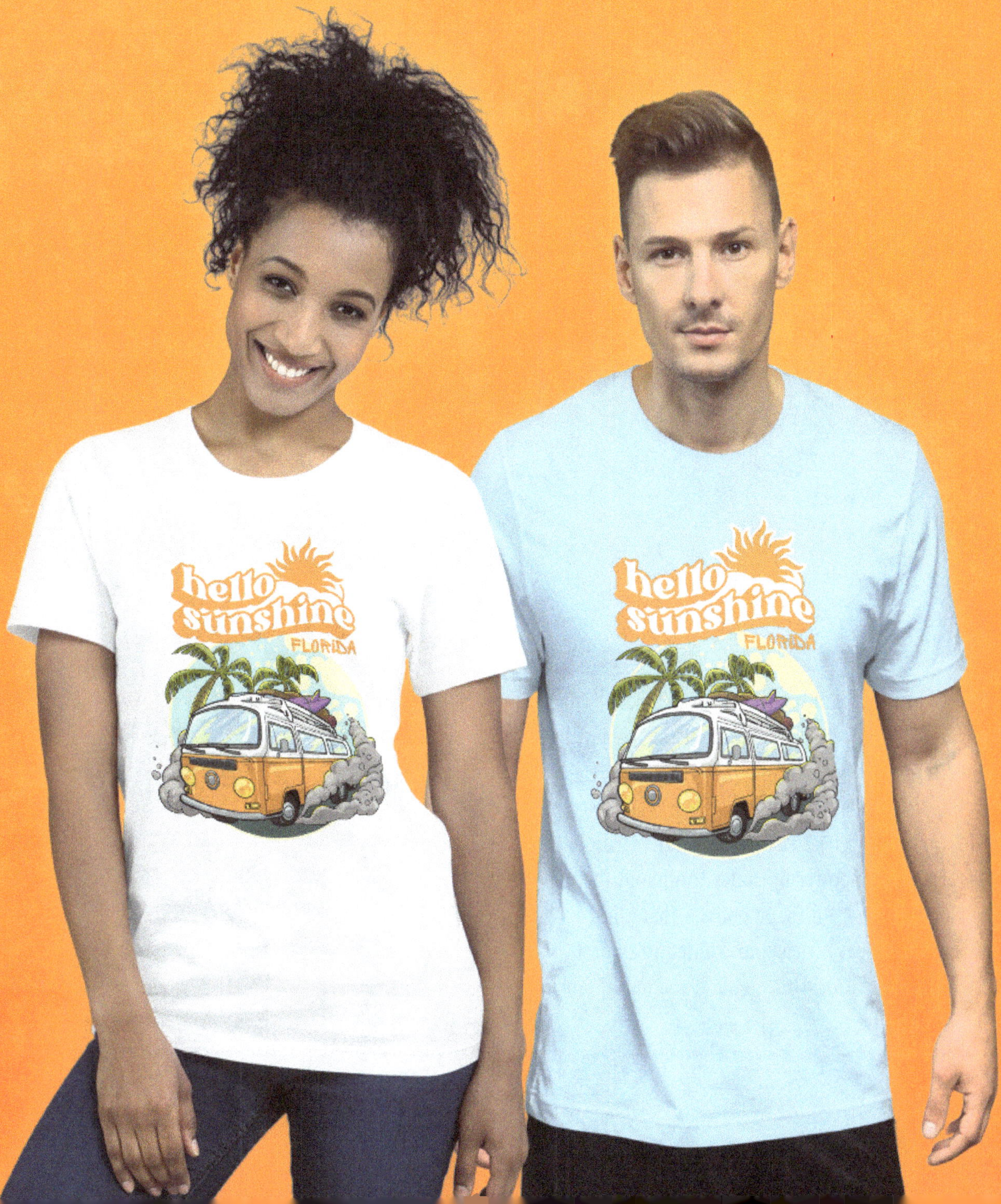

WHY ABORTION DECISIONS SHOULD REST WITH THE STATES

By Anil Anwar | Editor-In-Chief, Capitol Times Magazine

In recent remarks, former President Donald Trump reiterated his stance that decisions regarding abortion should be left to individual states.

This position reflects a fundamental principle of governance: empowering states to uphold the will of their citizens and shape policies that align with their values. It is a viewpoint rooted in respect for federalism, the Constitution, and the moral fabric of our nation.

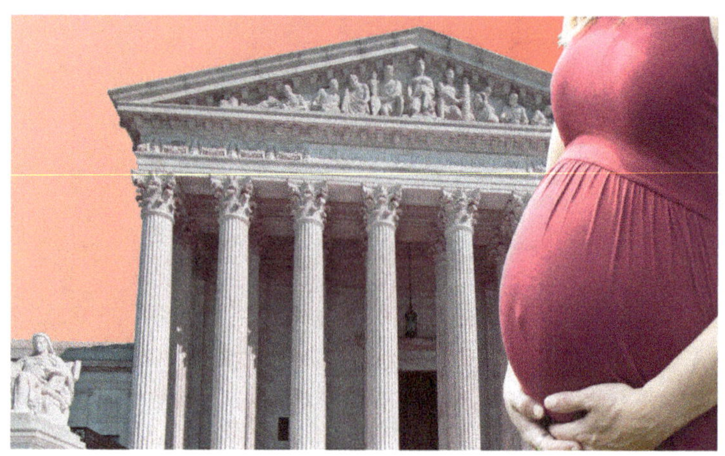

Donald Trump said on April 8 that decisions on abortion limitations should be left to states.

"My view is now that we have abortion where everyone wanted it from a legal standpoint, the states will determine by vote or legislation, or perhaps both. And whatever they decide must be the law of the land. In this case, the law of the state," Former President Trump said in a video posted on Truth Social, his social media platform.

"Many states will be different. Many will have a different number of weeks, or some will have more conservative than others, and that's what they will be. At the end of the day, this is all about the will of the people," Mr. Trump added.

President Trump rightly asserts that abortion is an issue where diversity of opinion and moral perspective is profound across our great nation. By allowing states to determine their own laws on abortion, we acknowledge and respect this diversity. What may be morally acceptable in one state may be deemed reprehensible in another. It is essential that our laws reflect the deeply held beliefs and values of the communities they serve.

Furthermore, this approach upholds the democratic process. The United States was founded on the principle of self-governance, where elected representatives enact laws that reflect the desires of their constituents. Allowing states to determine their abortion policies through legislation or a referendum ensures that the voice of the people is heard and respected.

Some may argue that abortion is a national issue requiring uniform standards across all states. However, the notion of a one-size-fits-all approach undermines the essence of federalism and disregards the cultural, religious, and ethical diversity that defines our nation. President Trump rightly acknowledges that each state is unique, with its own set of values and priorities. Therefore, decisions on such deeply personal matters should be made at the state level.

Critics of this approach argue for a centralized, national policy on abortion. They contend that this is necessary to protect the rights of unborn children and their mothers. However, the reality is that our nation remains deeply divided on this issue, and attempting to impose a singular federal policy would only exacerbate these divisions.

Moreover, recent legal developments, such as the landmark Dobbs v. Jackson Women's Health Organization decision, have shifted the landscape by allowing states greater latitude in regulating abortion. This empowers states to act in accordance with the values and priorities of their citizens without undue interference from the federal government.

Photo Source: reproductiverights.org | Dobbs v. Jackson Women's Health Organization

In light of recent discussions surrounding abortion policy, particularly the proposal for a national ban on abortions after 15 weeks, it is crucial for Christian conservatives to carefully consider the implications of such measures. While there is consensus among many Republicans, including former President Trump, on the need for limitations on abortion, there are important moral and practical considerations to address.

The sanctity of human life is a foundational principle within Christian conservatism. It is imperative that we advocate for policies that uphold and protect this fundamental value. The proposal to restrict abortions after 15 weeks reflects a growing recognition of the humanity of unborn children and the need to safeguard their right to life.

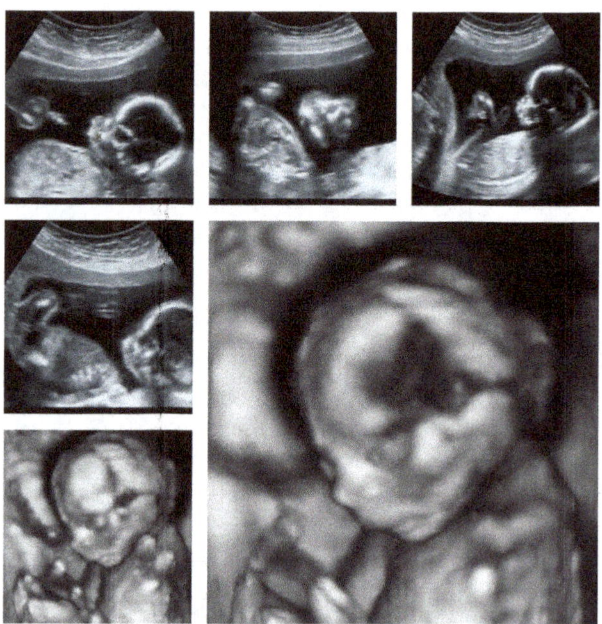

At the same time, as President Trump rightly noted, there is room for compassionate exceptions in cases of rape, incest, and when the life of the mother is at risk. These exceptions acknowledge the complexity of individual circumstances and ensure that our policies are guided by empathy and understanding.

However, it is also important to recognize the political realities at play. President Trump's acknowledgment that coming out too strongly against abortion could impact the 2024 election underscores the complexities of navigating this issue within our political landscape. While we must remain steadfast in our principles, we must also approach this issue with wisdom and discernment.

President Trump's assertion that abortion decisions should be left to the states is not only constitutionally sound but also morally principled. It recognizes the importance of local governance, respects the diversity of opinion within our nation, and upholds the democratic process. By allowing states to determine their own policies on abortion, we affirm the fundamental principles upon which our nation was founded: liberty, democracy, and respect for the rule of law.

As Christian conservatives, we also continue to advocate for policies that honor the sanctity of human life while also demonstrating compassion and understanding towards those facing difficult circumstances. It is our responsibility to engage in thoughtful dialogue and advocacy, ensuring that our policies reflect the values of faith, compassion, and respect for life. Let us remain steadfast in our commitment to protecting the most vulnerable among us and advancing a culture of life in our society.

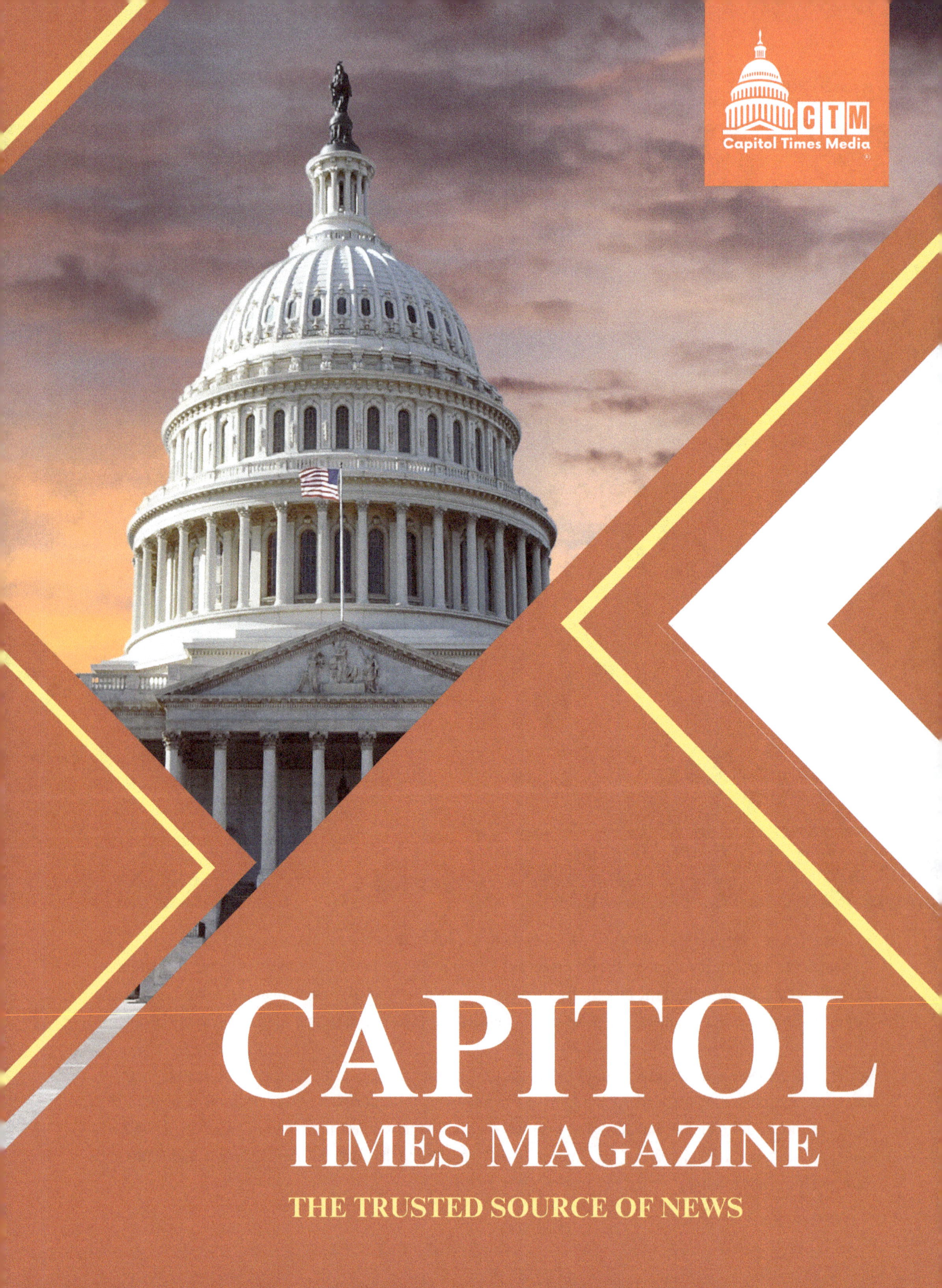

CTM
Capitol Times Media
CAPITOL
TIMES MAGAZINE
THE TRUSTED SOURCE OF NEWS

Ladies and gentlemen,

Welcome to Capitol Times Magazine. it is our privilege to bring you today's exclusive interview with a distinguished guest, a true American patriot, and a believer in Jesus Christ—Roger Stone.

As we delve into this conversation with Roger Stone, we have the opportunity to gain insights into his life, his beliefs, and his perspective on the critical issues facing our nation today. Roger Stone is not only a prominent figure in American politics but also someone who holds steadfast to his faith and values.

Join us as we explore Roger Stone's journey, his unwavering commitment to his convictions, and his vision for the future of our great nation. It is my hope that this dialogue will enlighten and inspire our readers, offering a unique glimpse into the mind of a remarkable individual who has left an indelible mark on the fabric of American politics.

Stay tuned for a thought-provoking and engaging conversation with Roger Stone—a man of principle, faith, and an unyielding belief in the promise of America.

Thank you for joining us on this captivating journey.

Warm regards,

Anil Anwar
Editor-in-Chief
Capitol Times Magazine

Interview with
ROGER STONE

A man of principle, faith, and an unyielding belief in the promise of America.

ANIL: *As a seasoned political operative with experience in thirteen national presidential campaigns, what do you think sets apart successful campaign strategies from unsuccessful ones?*

ROGER: As a veteran of thirteen national presidential campaigns, including those of Presidents Richard Nixon, Ronald Reagan, and Donald Trump, I believe the single most important quality that a successful presidential campaign must have is central control.

The essential guidelines for a campaign for President are the same as they are for a successful modern campaign for any public office.

While a candidate for President must avoid the temptation to manage his or her own campaign, the candidate must give full unilateral authority to one person and then support that person's decisions. A campaign that has factions or internal disagreement will invariably fail. That does not mean that all viewpoints should be heard and evaluated within the campaign structure, but once strategic decisions are made, all of those involved must support and help implement those decisions.

Political campaign structures are not a democracy and must, after full internal discussion, be a dictatorship in which the campaign moves with unity of purpose and speaks with one voice. A candidate who allows campaign staffers, supporters, or donors to circumvent the internal decision-making process of their campaign, will surely lose.

As a general rule of thumb, at least 80% of campaign resources must be spent on direct voter contact. These can include network television, cable television, terrestrial radio, voter mailings, blast e-mails, blast text messages, and live phone calls, as well as paid digital advertising. While social media is an effective way to communicate with activists, opinion leaders, donors, and other political elites, it is both an ineffective and inefficient way to communicate with voters.

Every successful campaign must begin with an in-depth benchmark poll to gauge voter attitudes and to pre-test ideas, themes, and initiatives, to measure the potential impact of each. While determining the status of the head-to-head trial heat, it is important to implement sophisticated polling in the testing, selection and formulation of key messages and themes for a successful campaign.

Such a benchmark poll is also invaluable in determining exactly how voters are getting their information. Campaign spending on mass communications should be determined based on this poll; in other words, if 78% of Republican primary voters say they are watching Fox News, one would be wise to purchase paid advertising at Fox News; if a majority of voters say they are deriving their news from very specific radio stations, buying advertising on those very stations would be a wise strategic decision. Determining how and where voters get their news is a vital step in planning and budgeting a successful campaign.

A successful campaign must also have the discipline to keep campaign overhead to less than 20% of campaign spending, as well as conserving resources for maximum expenditure in the last 30-45 days before the actual election contest. It remains true that most voters do not focus on either primaries or elections until the period just before voting begins. A successful campaign will carefully husband resources for expenditure during this period in an effort to be, at least, competitive with the campaign of your opponent.

A successful political campaign must also involve message discipline. In any given campaign, the candidate who dominates the dialogue and determines by their own messaging what the campaign will be about, will be successful. Just as in a commercial setting, repetition of a limited number of pre-tested, understandable messages are key to forming voter attitudes and opinions and winning actual votes.

ANIL: *Your work has spanned decades and administrations. What fundamental changes have you observed in the political landscape over the years?*

ROGER: Just as the advent of network television changed how voters got their news, the advent and proliferation of internet communications has revolutionized politics. That said, it is important to note that while recent polling indicated that the vast majority of voters are getting their information digitally, that does not necessarily mean that they are getting it through social media platforms.

The internet revolution has made the overall cost of an effective political campaign more affordable. Prior to being able to reach voters relatively inexpensively through the internet, only those campaigns able to purchase heavy advertising on network television, cable television, and radio could be effective and victorious. While paid targeted advertising through Facebook can be extremely effective, it is important to note that Facebook often restricts the ability to purchase such advertising when it comes to Republican and conservative candidates.

At the same time, the advent of the internet means that all news is immediate. The maturity of a free, fair, and uncensored internet in 2016 allowed for the election of a political outsider, Donald Trump, who was not the favorite of political and media elites. That also explains why we now know that agencies within the U.S. government worked

hand in glove with tech giants such as Google, YouTube, Twitter, Facebook, and Instagram, among others, to restrict, censor, and, in some cases, cancel political messaging that was contrary to the accepted narrative of the government and media combine.

This censorship, particularly on the part of Google, which have regulated what we can and cannot see in our e-mail boxes, as well as what information is elevated in internet searches (as well as determining what information shall be suppressed), played a crucial role in fostering the accepted narrative during the COVID-19 pandemic, as well as delegitimizing any reasonable and fact-based questions regarding the outcome of the 2020 election.

ANIL: *Could you share a memorable experience from your time as campaign aide to President Nixon?*

ROGER: My favorite memory of my time with President Nixon dates to his post-presidential years.

President Nixon made a mean martini and was quite proud of his martini-mixing skills, calling them "Silver Bullet." Gin was the old man's preference, over vodka. I myself am a vodka man. Undoubtedly, Nixon honed his mixology skills tending bar at "Nick's Hamburger Stand," an impromptu canteen put together by the enterprising Navy lieutenant for war-weary service members passing through Nixon's post in the South Pacific in World War II. Dick served up booze and burgers. Nixon served at Guadalcanal and later at

Green Island as an officer in charge of the South Pacific Combat Air Transport Command, supervising C-47 cargo operations. Lieutenant Commander Nixon was legendary for his ability to acquire "hooch" for the boys. It was through his pop-up hamburger stand and his poker winnings that Nixon compiled the modest nest egg that would initially finance his 1946 campaign for Congress.

Generally speaking, Nixon was not introspective. He hated to talk about the past, always looking forward instead. It was hard to get him to talk about Ike, McCarthy, JFK, LBJ, and the deep secrets he held close for so many decades. But after two drinks, the old man became absolutely loquacious and would reveal astonishing things, cloaked in Nixonian intrigue, of course.

"More than one of these and you want to beat your wife," Nixon reportedly told his then-26-year-old assistant John P. Sears.

The coolest thing about Nixon's "Silver Bullet" was that it was handed down to Nixon from no less a legend than British Prime Minister and wartime leader Winston Churchill.

DICK NIXON'S SILVER BULLET MARTINI RECIPE.

Ingredients:
- One (1) bottle of small to medium sized green olives with pimento.
- Dry Vermouth of choice.
- Fine Russian vodka (or Tanqueray gin, as Nixon preferred)

Assembly:
- Drain the brine from the bottle of olives, leaving olives intact.
- Refill olive bottle with water; shake vigorously; drain water completely.
- Refill olive bottle with dry Vermouth; refrigerate the bottle.
- Chill a traditional martini glass.
- Fill a cocktail shaker with ice, preferably a vintage Tiffany hammered silver art deco shaker.
- Fill the shaker with vodka (or gin, according to preference) until the ice is covered.
- Shake VERY vigorously—if there are not tiny shards of ice floating on the surface of the Silver Bullet, you have not shaken the mixture vigorously enough.
- Pour the mixture into the chilled martini glass.
- Add one Vermouth-drenched olive from the jar.
- Return the Vermouth olive jar to the refrigerator for use with your next Silver Bullet.

ANIL: *What do you believe are the key qualities that make a successful leader in today's political environment?*

ROGER: Having known and worked for four American Presidents, as well as longtime Senate Republican Leader Bob Dole, I think the single most important quality in a leader is courage. Our most successful Presidents and political leaders have been those individuals with the courage, strength, and conviction to take important political positions that are contrary to the powerful, entrenched interests within both government and society. The courage to make and stick with unpopular decisions when you believe they are correct is paramount. It would be a misnomer to believe that our American political system is divided by two major parties with polar opposite views. While I have a longtime sentimental attachment to the Republican Party, as the party of Lincoln, Eisenhower, Nixon, Reagan, and Trump, I have come to the sad conclusion that the leadership of both major parties are dominated by an entrenched ruling elite that consists of unelected bureaucrats in all branches of government, as well as monied interests that dominate the media, mass communications, and economies around the world.

Few Presidents have had the courage and the fortitude to stand up to these interests. President John F. Kennedy opposed those who wanted to provoke a deadly war with Russia, opposed a silver-backed dollar, opposed a nuclear Israel, and opposed our presence in Vietnam. JFK was murdered because he had the courage to buck the military-industrial complex that favored war, paper money, and expanded foreign adventurism.

President Richard Nixon was removed from office largely because of his planned intention to curb the influence and power of the intelligence agencies, as well as the Pentagon. Nixon knew that the Ivy League elitist who dominated the CIA preferred the more cultured JFK whom they deemed to be sufficiently anti-communist, over Nixon in 1960 and deeply resented the agency's briefing of JFK regarding the planned Bay of Pigs invasion before the first debate in the 1960 campaign. Kennedy would successfully exploit this tip-off to Nixon's detriment in the Chicago debate, taunting Eisenhower as Vice President for being insufficiently committed to the removal of Fidel Castro, all the while JFK knew that there was a plan afoot to remove the Cuban dictator, which Nixon could not reveal as a matter of national security. Nixon also had clashed with the CIA over their refusal to give him the documentation of their role in Kennedy's murder.

Only months ago, Politico reported on a rarely noted Watergate era tape recording of President Richard Nixon in the Oval Office with CIA Director Richard Helms, in which our 37th President can clearly be heard threatening the CIA Director by saying, "I know who shot John."

President Donald Trump survived an illegitimate investigation into his campaign based on fabricated evidence of "Russian collusion," as well as two completely fabricated impeachment attempts—all fostered by his refusal to plunge America deeper into the endless foreign wars that had been so profitable for the deep state war machine.

The willful targeting of Donald Trump and his campaign, in which the full authority of the U.S. government and the incredible capabilities of both U.S. and foreign intelligence, utilizing what the FBI and CIA both knew was fabricated evidence contained in the Steele Dossier to justify FISA warrants to spy on officials in Trump's campaign, as well as surveilling Trump himself, is the greatest single abuse of power in American history. We now know that even prior to using the X Steele Dossier to justify the issuing of FISA warrants, CIA Director John Brennan asked multiple foreign intelligence services to surveill and "bump," which essentially means entrap, 26 associates of Donald Trump without any probable cause of any illegal activity.

We also now know, definitively, based on the long-delayed report by Special Counsel John Durham, that there was no collusion between Russian intelligence and the Trump campaign. Democrats and many in the mainstream media repeatedly falsely insist that Trump Campaign Manager Paul Manafort shared proprietary polling information from the Trump campaign with a man named Konstantin Kilimnik. The problem with this assertion is that it is false.

In fact, despite their heavily taxpayer-funded and media-fueled investigation, the only alleged evidence that both House Intelligence Committee Chairman Adam Schiff and de facto Special Counsel Andrew Weissmann constantly cite is this false allegation about Kilimnik.

There are two fundamental problems with this phony narrative. First is the substantial evidence that not only is Kilimnik not a Russian intelligence asset, but evidence shows that he was working extensively with US Intelligence. Kilimnik actually worked for US Senator John McCain prior to the 2016 Presidential Campaign.

Paul Manafort himself addressed this in his book, "Political Prisoner: Persecuted, Prosecuted, but Not Silenced" when he said, "…my associate Konstantin Kilimnik…. was not only not a Russian agent, but he was a US asset. He was so important to the US embassy in Kiev that he had a code name to protect him in cable traffic between Ukraine and Washington." Manafort went on to say that "The same anonymous US government sources who pushed this false narrative had access to the State Department files that identified him as a valued asset. They knew he was not a spy."

Independent journalist Matt Taibbi reported, "The FBI's own declassified reports show Kilimnik met with the head of the Kiev embassy's political section "at least biweekly" during his time working with Manafort and Yanukovitch, adding that he "displayed good knowledge and seemed to know what was going on," and came across as "less slanted" than other sources, among many other things. This fits with what I was told by multiple former colleagues of Kilimnik's, that staffers in the Kiev embassy valued his analyses above those of some Americans in Yanukovitch's orbit. Taibbi also noted that Kilimnik was so valued as a source by the State Department that his name was redacted from classified cables to and from the U.S. embassy in Kiev.

The other major problem with this false claim of Russian collusion with the Trump campaign and that Manafort passed highly secret polling to this alleged Russian agent is the fact that Manafort had no poll numbers that were proprietary to the Trump campaign at the time both Democrats and Federal prosecutors claimed he had shared the data with Kilimnik.

Again Manafort wrote, "The major misrepresentation by Weissman related to the "secret internal" polling data that I supposedly gave to Kilimnik. The fact that the campaign polling that I supposedly gave Kilimnik at the August 2 meeting was not even completed until August 8 was ignored. Also, ignored, was (Manfort Deputy Rick) Gates's testimony in his proffers to the FBI that the information that he gave to Kilimnik was publicly available information.

The significance is that the campaign had no non-public polling data on August 2. Republican Pollster Tony Fabrizio, who was working for Trump had gone into the field in the battleground states on Aug 1 with the preliminary results not becoming available to me or Gates until Aug 8 and later." There was no Russian Collusion with the Trump campaign. No passing of poll numbers by Manafort nor in the release of the Wikileaks disclosures regarding Hillary and her campaign nor in the Trump Tower meeting with Donald Trump, Jr. and others who met with a Russian Woman lawyer who was briefed before and after her meeting by her handlers at Fusion-GPS, the creators of the fabricated Steele Dossier.

ANIL: *Your book "The Man Who Killed Kennedy: The Case Against LBJ" sparked controversy. What inspired you to delve into this particular aspect of history?*

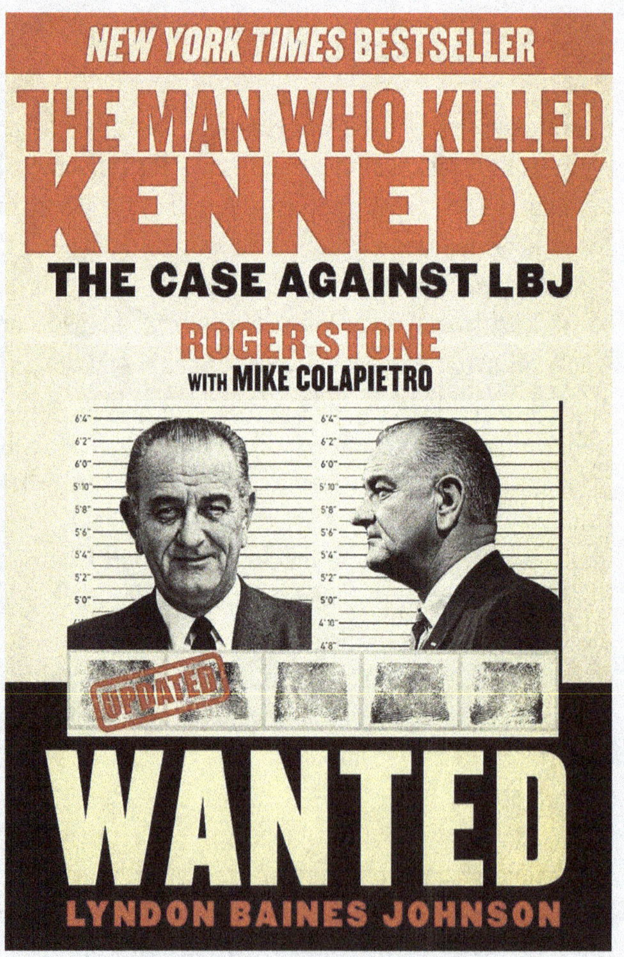

ROGER: I became interested in politics in 1963 when the woman who lived next door to my family gave me a copy of Senator Barry Goldwater's book "Conscience of a Conservative".

I immediately became a Goldwater zealot and began volunteering at the local Republican headquarters for his presidential campaign. It is during that campaign that I first read a book, A Texan Looks at Lyndon by J. Evetts Haley, which was a shocking exposé of the epic corruption of Senator, Vice President, and President, Lyndon Baines Johnson, who became President upon the Dallas-based murder of President John F. Kennedy. While this shocking paperback book was read by millions of Americans, the mainstream media of the day largely concealed the extraordinary greed, corruption, duplicity, cowardice, and racist reality regarding LBJ.

Like most Americans, I initially accepted the hasty and immediate conclusions of the Warren Commission, which was appointed by President Lyndon Johnson to investigate the murder of President Kennedy. By 1996, I had read important books by L. Fletcher Prouty, Gaeton Fonzi, Jim Marrs, and Mark Lane—raising fundamental questions about the conclusion of the Warren Commission that Lee Harvey Oswald, a disgruntled communist, was solely responsible for the murder of JFK, firing three bullets, all from behind, from the sixth-floor window of the Texas School Book Depository Building.

This fostered my fundamental disbelief in the government-promoted "official" explanation of President Kennedy's murder that was pushed so relentlessly by the media, who also sought to silence or discredit any researcher, historian, author, or citizen who challenged this narrative.

Having gleaned a fundamental distrust and suspicion regarding Lyndon Johnson from my earlier reading, I then read The Texas Connection: The Assassination of President John F. Kennedy by Craig I. Zirbel, as well as Blood, Money, & Power: How LBJ Killed JFK by Barr McClellan, and LBJ and the Kennedy Killing by assasintion eyewitness James T. Tague. The basic outline of Johnson's motive, means, and opportunity for the murder of JFK is thoroughly documented in these books—all of which are fully attributed and accredited within my book, **The Man Who Killed Kennedy: The Case Against LBJ.**

It was not, however, until a private conversation I had with former President Richard Nixon in his post-presidential years, that I decided to write my book on the Kennedy assasination which would become a New York Times Best Seller. Asked over cocktails who really killed John F. Kennedy, President Richard Nixon first said, "The Warren Commission is the biggest goddam hoax in American history," before he said, "Let's put it this way: Lindon and I both wanted to be President—the difference was, I wasn't willing to kill for it."

This conversation motivated me to conduct my own research, including interviews with the aforementioned authors, Barr McClellan and the late James T. Tague, as well as researching the relationship between Dallas nightclub owner Jack Ruby, who murdered alleged assassin Lee Harvey Oswald in cold blood on national television, and Lyndon Johnson.

In my book, which is very heavily footnoted and referenced, I used eyewitness and fingerprint evidence, as well as deep Texas politics, to make the case that Lyndon Johnson orchestrated a conspiracy to murder President John F. Kennedy in order to avoid public disgrace and prosecution for massive crimes of corruption that would have not only removed him from the 1964 Democratic ticket but also sent him to prison. It should be noted that I do not claim that LBJ alone arranged the assassination of John F. Kennedy on November 22, 1963, but rather that he was at the helm of a conspiracy that included others who had their own distinct interest in Kennedy's death and the succession to the presidency of Lyndon Baines Johnson.

ANIL: *How do you respond to critics who may challenge your conclusions about the JFK assassination?*

ROGER: Let me be clear that the premise of my book is not that LBJ orchestrated the murder of his predecessor to the exclusion of all the other entities and powers who had an interest in Kennedy's murder and removal from the presidency. Indeed, I believe Johnson was at the helm of a carefully orchestrated plot to kill Kennedy, which included the CIA, organized crime, Big Texas Oil, the Pentagon, the Secret Service, and the banking interests.

My research led me to conclude that while the FBI was not directly involved in the plot to kill Kennedy, FBI Director J. Edgar Hoover, who was an intimate of Johnson's, had a direct interest in the plot's success; Hoover, who was considered a crusty anachronism by the Kennedy brothers, would hit mandatory federal retirement age in 1964, and the veteran G-Man knew that JFK would cashier him once reelected. After the success of the plot to kill Kennedy, Hoover moved aggressively to cover up the truth regarding

Kennedy's death. Hoover opened and closed the FBI's investigation of the murder in less than seven days and cemented the narrative that Lee Harvey Oswald, a lone nut, was solely responsible for Kennedy's murder, having fired three shots from the sixth-floor window of the Texas School Book Depository Building. The charge of the Warren Commission, reluctantly chaired by U.S. Supreme Court Chief Justice Earl Warren, was to essentially rubberstamp the FBI's flawed "conclusions."

One of the great flaws in earlier conclusions by researchers examining the Kennedy assasination is that they viewed Kennedy's murder through the limited prism of the motives of each of these individual power centers. In other words, for example, those steeped in the history and actions of organized crime, such as those who staffed and ran the United States House of Representatives Select Committee on Assassinations in 1976, reach the incomplete conclusion that the mob was responsible for Kennedy's death as payback for the Kennedy brothers' betrayal of the mafia, who had played a key role in financing and helping to steal the 1960 election for JFK, only to have Attorney General Robert F. Kennedy seek deportation of mob chieftains Carlos Marcello and Santo Trafficante Jr. It is not that their conclusion that the mob murdered Kennedy is wrong, it is that it is incomplete. By the same token, those more familiar with the history and actions of the CIA would believe that the agency was solely responsible for Kennedy's murder.

The CIA supported the removal of JFK because they believed that he bungled the failed Bay of Pigs invasion of Cuba, as well as mishandling the Cuban Missile Crisis. The CIA was also concerned that JFK was showing increased skepticism regarding America's deeper involvement and commitment in Vietnam at the time of his death.

Kennedy similarly enraged Big Texas Oil with his support for the elimination of the Oil Depletion Allowance, which allowed the Texas oil barons to avoid millions of dollars in federal taxes. Kennedy's insistence on a silver-backed dollar similarly outraged the banking interests, who were eager to move the U.S. dollar to a paper-backed currency.

Based on the research of those who came before me and bolstered by my own independent research, I believe that John F. Kennedy was shot from both the front and the back by multiple shooters. I have effectively debunked the scientifically-impossible "single-bullet theory" that holds that one of the three bullets shot by Lee Harvey Oslwald passed through JFK and subsequently wounded Texas Governor John Connely. I also reject the assertion that the fleeing Lee Harvery Oswald shot and killed Dallas police officer J. D. Tippit. Indeed, the spent shells found on the ground at the site of Tippit's murder were fired from an automatic, while Lee Harvey Oswald was apprehended in a nearby Dallas movie theater brandishing a revolver. It is also crucial to note that a paraffin test administered to Oswald by the Dallas Police Department showed no traces of nitrates on his chest or body, impossible if he had fired a leaky World War II vintage Italian carbine that day.

In my book, The Man Who Killed Kennedy: The Case Against LBJ, I meticulously document the motive and role of each of these entities in Kennedy's death. However, I also make the compelling case that it was Lyndon Johnson who had the greatest and most immediate interest in killing Kennedy and replacing him as President.

In my New York Times Best Seller, I use fingerprint evidence found on the sixth-floor of the Texas School Book Depository Building to identify at least one of the shooters of JFK as Malcolm "Mac" Wallace, whose relationship with LBJ I fully document.

I also reveal, in my book, that legendary CIA operative E. Howard Hunt, later arrested as one of the Watergate burglars, confided to his son, Saint John Hunt, on his deathbed, that he had been in Dallas on November 22nd, 1963 and that "Lyndon Johnson was running the show" for what he called, "the big event."

I strongly urge those who doubt my thesis that LBJ orchestrated the murder of John F. Kennedy to read my book, **The Man Who Killed Kennedy: The Case Against LBJ.** As they say in Latin, "Cui bono?" or "Who benefits?"

stonezone.com/product/the-man-who-killed-kennedy-the-case-against-lbj-signed-paperback/

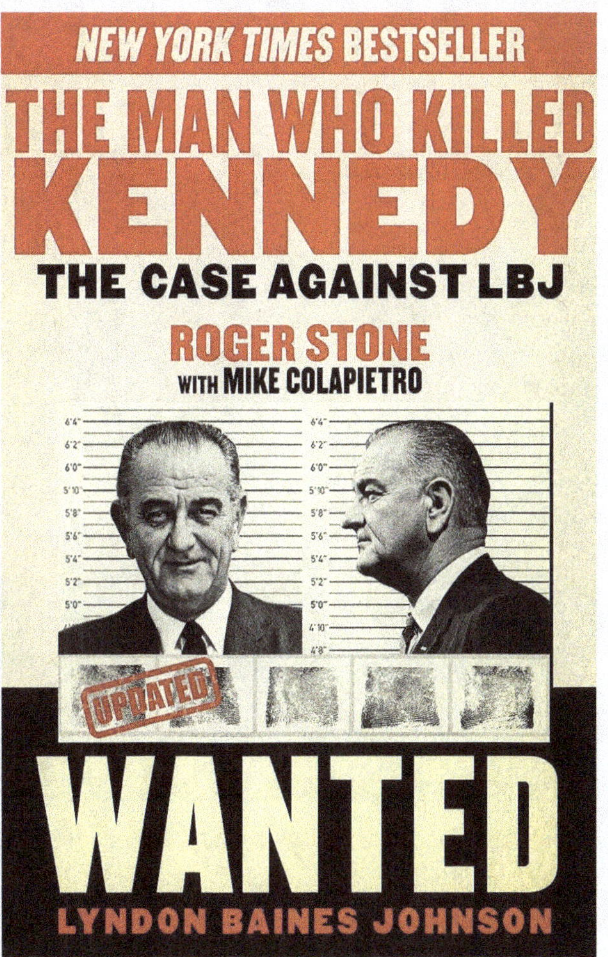

ANIL: *What motivated you to write "The Clinton's War on Women" and "The Bush Crime Family"? What message did you aim to convey through these works?*

ROGER: <u>The Clintons' War on Women</u> is probably the most accurate and detailed compendium of the epic corruption and extraordinary evil of Bill and Hillary Clinton. In fact, I was the first American author to fully expose the identity and role of child sex predator and sex trafficker, Jeffrey Epstein.

stonezone.com/product/the-clintons-war-on-women-signed-paperback/

I note that Chapter 8, "Orgy Island," is both the longest chapter in the book and it includes the FAA flight logs which first detailed the identities of luminaries, celebrities, business leaders, and academics who visited Epstein's island. The book also reveals Bill Clinton's record of vicious sexual assault and rape against as many as 38 women, as well as fully exposing Hillary Clinton's role in selecting the

heavy-handed detectives and vicious lawyers who saught to cover-up Bill Clinton's brutal crimes. I have no doubt that my authorship of this shocking book, on the eve of the 2016 election, was a major motivation for my subsequent prosecution for entirely fabricated process crimes by Special Counsel Robert Mueller; every one of the vicious, partisan prosecutors in my case had worked previously for Hillary Clinton.

In 1980, I worked for former California Governor Ronald Reagan, specifically charged with winning the Republican primaries in New York, Connecticut, and New Jersey. It was there that I first encountered the reality of the Bush family. While the Bushes seemed genial in their outward demeanor, they had an elitist attitude toward those who were not as privileged as they were, and a deep sense of entitlement when it came to the 1980 Republican presidential nomination. That under my direction Reagan would sweep every delegate in the Republican primaries in New York and New Jersey, while winning the delegates in three out of six of Connecticuts' congressional districts, splitting the Connecticut delegates 16 for Bush and 15 for Reagan, would earn me the undying enmity of family matriarch Barbara Bush. Completely contrary to her claims in a biography published just before her death in which the former First Lady insisted that she learned that I had been hired for Bush's 1988 campaign and had successfully demanded that I be fired, in fact, I never worked for George H. W. Bush in 1988 and instead supported the candidacy of upstate New York Congressman Jack Kemp for that year's presidential nomination. I attribute Barbara Bush's inaccurate memory to her heavy drinking.

After Reagan was nominated, all members of Reagan's senior political staff were called to a meeting to voice our opinions about who the Gipper should choose as his vice-presidential running mate. Not a single member of the Reagan senior campaign staff favored the selection of George H. W. Bush. Several supported the selection of Nevada U.S. Senator Paul Laxalt, who was a solid conservative and Reagan loyalist, while the majority favored the selection of Buffalo-area Congressman Jack

Kemp, an early advocate of tax cuts and supply-side economics who had been an important early supporter of Reagan's candidacy. Kemp's prospects for the ticket were destroyed by a vicious campaign of rumor and innuendo regarding his private life that was generated by the Bush camp. The selection of Bush by Reagan could have been his largest single error.

My book about the Bushes, **The Bush Crime Family**, is a shocking true story of privilege, ambition, eugenics, criminal fraud in the S&L industry, drug trafficking, pedophilia, adultry, and assasination. The Bush family fortune was made by patriarch Prescott Bush - a partner at the Wall Street investment firm Brown Brothers Harriman & Co., who served as Adolf Hitler's personal banker, and who arranged the financing for the armament of Hitler's Third Reich. Shortly after I published my 2016 book documenting Prescott Bush's role as the financier for the Nazi war machine, the documents which detail the federal government's seizure of the Bush-owned, New York-based Union Banking Corporation disappeared from the National Archives.

stonezone.com/product/the-bush-crime-family-the-inside-story-of-an-american-dynasty/

That I would write books sharply critical of both the Clintons and the Bushes demonstrates that I am not some lockstep Republican. In fact, I believe that George H. W. Bush's ascension to the presidency marked the end of the revolution in the Republican Party, in which control of the GOP was ripped from the eastern elites through the nomination of Senator Barry Goldwater in 1964 and was completed by the nomination and election of Ronald Reagan in 1980. Donald Trump's nomination in 2016 is nothing less than the highjacking of the Republican Party from the neocon elites who came to control the party after the election of Bush, and who dictated the failed nominations of neocons John McCain and Mitt Romney.

Above all, I ask those who question the thesis of either **The Clinton's War on Women** or **The Bush Crime Family** to read each book thoroughly before passing judgment on my scholarship.

ANIL: *Can you shed some light on the process of writing your New York Times bestsellers, particularly "The Making of the President 2016"?*

ROGER: My book, **The Making of the President 2016: How Donald Trump Orchestrated a Revolution,** is a blow-by-blow account of both Donald Trump's improbable nomination in 2016, as well as his upset election over Hillary Clinton. I would remind your readers that on October 18th, 2016, The New York Times reported that there was a "91% chance" that Hillary Clinton would be elected based on their analysis of polling just before the election.

I have been a friend and advisor to President Donald Trump for 45-years. I was among the first people in the country to urge him to seriously consider a presidential bid. In fact, I first urged him to seek the presidency in 1988. Interestingly, the first major political figure who recognized Trump's strengths as an independent thinker, as well as his extraordinary skills as a communicator, was former President Richard Nixon. After meeting Trump in the Owner's Box at Yankee Stadium on opening day in 1987, Nixon would pen a letter to the future President, telling him, "Whenever you decide to run for office you will be a winner!"

stonezone.com/product/the-making-of-the-president-2016/

People who see Trump's afable and sometimes amusing public persona, or who underestimate the power of his simple belief in policies that put America first, fail to recognize the innate toughness of Donald Trump. The Trump I know is an amazingly resilient, determined, confident, and resourceful leader. Trump has benefited his entire career from being underestimated. I believe that he is being underestimated even today, and that he will overcome the relentless smears of the mainstream media and the current weaponization of our criminal justice system, to return to the White House in January of 2025.

ANIL: *With your experience as Chairman of Donald Trump's Presidential Exploratory Committee in 2000, how do you perceive his political evolution over the years?*

Photo Source: Roger Stone Facebook

ROGER: I think it is vital to understand that even as a former President, Donald Trump is not, and never will be, a "politician." Trump is the leader of a political movement which he readily conceded is much larger than Trump himself. The rules that have governed the advancement of other conventional political figures are simply not valid when it comes to Donald Trump.

Despite his Ivy League education where he excelled at his studies at the Wharton School of Finance, Trump is not and will never be an elitist. Despite his status as a billionaire, with extraordinary success in the cutthroat world of Manhattan real-estate, Trump has never lost his understanding and appreciation for the middle class working people of America.

ANIL: *What are some of the most common misconceptions people have about political consulting and strategizing?*

ROGER: Some people believe that a campaign can be waged without first conducting a benchmark poll to determine voter attitudes from a scientifically drawn sample of the voters in the jurisdiction in which you will be running. Waging a campaign without first doing this basic research would be akin to driving a car with your eyes closed; you do know you will go forward, but you have no idea what you might hit.

Candidates who eschew this kind of initial professional research because they "know what the voters think" or act on the basis of anecdotal information, are normally called "losers."

Another huge misconception is that billboards or yard signs win elections. Since such signage can only, by definition, communicate your name, they are of extremely limited utility in terms of persuading people to vote for you. Both may be necessary to bolster the morale of your campaign volunteers and donors, but neither will actually win you votes.

At the same time, it is vital to recognize that any campaign for public office must be based on sophisticated polling (survey research) designed to determine the current attitude of voters, as well as the voters' potential reaction to events, issue positions, or other initiatives the campaign might undertake.

An effective, efficient, and victorious political campaign must be entirely data-driven. Any campaign that proceeds without an initial benchmark poll, substituting hunches, theories, or opinions regarding the dynamics of the race and the attitude of the voters, is doomed to fail.

ANIL: *How has your experience working with multiple Republican presidents influenced your political ideology and strategy?*

ROGER: While all of the Republican Presidents and presidential candidates I have worked for share certain

common traits and characteristics, each is also individual in their own talents and strengths. Trump, like Reagan, is a "big picture" leader who is focused largely on the key elements of his messaging, while Nixon had a tendency to micromanage every aspect of both his campaign and presidency.

Nixon, Reagan, and Trump all recognized the important light under which their candidacies and presidencies would be viewed. Each of them understood the importance of appearing calm, confident, and strong as a way to inspire both their supporters and the American people.

ANIL: *In your opinion, what are the most pressing issues facing the United States today, and how do you propose they be addressed?*

ROGER: There is quite obviously no more pressing and urgent problem than the invasion of the United Stated by as many as 25 million illegal migrants. This flood of illegal migrants has brought with it a fentanyl epidemic, as well as a spike in crime across the country. It has also driven states, cities, and counties to the edge of fiscal bankruptcy, as state and local governments struggle to pay for the legally required social services for the illegals who are being efficiently farmed out from our Southern Border. It is not incidental that the liberal Democrat mayors of New York City and Chicago have already said that the current situation is unsustainable and financial ruin is imminent.

The migrant invasion that has been accelerated by what is essentially the open-borders policy of the Biden Administration has not just flooded America with illegals from Central and South America. Without any doubt, there has been an enormous invasion of military-age single males from China and the Middle East. How many dangerous terrorists have been admitted to the country? When will there be a shocking terrorist attack on American soil?

The only answer is the immediate enforcement of the laws already on the books to seal our Southern Border—these are the very laws and regulations that President Joe Biden suspended upon his election. Secondarily, we require the mass deportation of the millions who have come to America illegally. President Dwight Eisenhower efficiently **deported 1.3 million illegals** during his administration - President Donald Trump has pledged to enact this same type of legal deportation of those who have come to America illegally. It both can, and must, be done.

ANIL: *What significance do you see in Chris Christie selecting Ellis Henican, who you've described as a "left-wing Reagan hater," as his ghostwriter, particularly in the context of his political background and affiliations?*

ROGER: Given that I ran Ronald Reagn's campaign in New Jersey in both 1980 and 1984, I can attest to the fact that young Chris Christie was never a Reagan supporter. Nor is Chris Christie, by any measure, a reliable conservative. The very idea that Chris Christie would now produce a ghostwritten book lionising Ronald Reagan is preposterous. That Christie would select veteran left-wing Newsday columnist Ellis Henican, who is a vociferous hater of both Ronald Reagan and Donald Trump, speaks volumes about the hypocrisy of Christie's book which I predict will not sell very well.

ANIL: *Your recent statement regarding Bill Kristol has garnered attention. Could you elaborate on your criticisms of him and why you believe he is responsible for the deaths in the Iraq war?*

ROGER: As the chief of staff for Vice President Dick Cheney, Bill Kristol was a key actor in the promulgation of the false narrative that Saddam Hussein had weapons of mass destruction and had played some role in the attacks on America by Islamist terrorists on 9/11. Both of these falsehoods were used to rationalize the brutal war in Iraq, in which over **1 million** people lost their lives. We now know that this rationale was not only fabricated, but that National Security Advisor Colin Powell was forced by Cheney to lie about it in a dramatic presentation to the United Nations.

Kristol is an unreconstructed neocon who has relentlessly supported endless foreign wars, where the inherent interests of the United States are neither clear nor convincing. Neocons like Kristol seized and controlled both major parties until the election of Donald Trump, who got elected specifically on a platform of ending America's costly foreign wars and starting no new wars. This is precisely why Kristol and his ilk have been so vicious in their attacks on Trump. Indeed, as President, Trump would quickly resolve the Ukraine-Russia war, at the same time ending the Biden Administration's funding of Islamic terrorists in the Middle East by unfreezing billions in assets for Iran.

ANIL: *Congressman Jerry Nadler recently made allegations of a death threat from you, which he claims to have communicated to Capitol police and the FBI. What is your response to these accusations?*

ROGER: The claims echoed by Nadler are entirely false. Mediaite, a left-wing news site, produced a crude audio which they claimed came from an anonymous source and was recorded four years ago.

The audio purports to claim that I specifically threatened the lives of two Democrat congressmen, including Nadler. Immediate forensic examination of the audio in question, using two different sophisticated AI-detection software programs demonstrate that said audio is a fabrication created with the use of artificial intelligence.

Further examination shows that the ambient "restaurant background noise" was layered into the audio after the creation of the entirely AI-generated voice track, to further conceal the fabrication of the audio.

Needless to say, MSNBC, CNN, The New York Times, The Guardian, and the usual legacy media outlets immediately reported on the posting of this phony audio by Mediaite without any reasonable examination of the authenticity of the audio itself.

I debunked this hitjob by the same people who insisted, falsely, that I was a "Russian intelligence asset," as well as an "intermediary between Trump and WikiLeaks," here. *https://stonezone.com/roger-stone-assassination-audio-debunked-rare/*

In 2019, I was falsely charged by Special Counsel Robert Mueller with lying under oath in my voluntary testimony to the House Intelligence Committee. While I concede that I did make misstatements, none of these were either material nor did they conceal any underlying crime. In fact, government prosecutors never provided any actual evidence that I had either colluded with Russian intelligence or collaborated with WikiLeaks in their release of documents from the Democratic National Committee and the Clinton campaign (which U.S. intelligence agencies falsely claimed were obtained through an online hack of the DNC's computer servers).

In fact, the FBI admitted in discovery before my trial that they had never inspected the computer servers of the DNC and had relied entirely on a third-party, a left-leaning IT company called Crowdstrike, whose report alleged that the DNC had been the target of an online hack by the Russians. What we did not know during my trial is that Crowdstrike President Shawn Henry (who just happens to be a former Assistant to FBI Director Robert Mueller) actually testified under oath to the House Intelligence Committee and admitted that his company's report had no actual proof of this alleged online "Russian hack." After the FBI's embarrassing admission in my trial, DOJ prosecutors insisted, without proof, that they had additional evidence that would prove that the DNC had been hacked by the Russians but they never provided any because, in fact, there is none.

Mueller's prosecutors insisted that I be tried before Judge Amy Berman Jackson because they said my case was "related" to the so-called Russian hacking case which never even reached the discovery phase, and promised the judge that they would produce evidence against me at my trial collected from the warrants in that case. Again, they never provided any such evidence because none exists.

The real reason I was charged with these wholly fabricated crimes was to pressure me into offering false testimony against President Donald Trump. Mueller's prosecutors wanted me to testify, falsely, that I had discussed and even predicted the WikiLeaks disclosures in multiple phone conversations with candidate Trump in 2016. I refused to lie in this regard and thus was subjected to a Soviet-style show trial in Washington D.C., in which my constitutional rights were violated and in which I was not allowed to put forward forensic evidence or expert testimony that would prove that the underlying premise of my indictment, that "the Russians had hacked the DNC," was false.

Equally innocuous was my one and only Twitter Direct Message exchange with a flack for WikiLeaks, which is also innocuous in its content in that it, once again, provided no evidence of cooperation, collusion, or collaboration. Assange himself said, in multiple interviews, that WikiLeaks had never provided me with any material whatsoever from their sources. Once again, the fake news media and their allies in the Justice Department made much of communications that are both limited and benign on their face.

Both Mueller and the bloodthirsty fake news media made much of an innocuous Twitter Direct Message exchange between me and the online persona of "Guccifer 2.0." The Department of Justice and the CIA insisted that Guccifer 2.0 was a "Russian hacker" responsible for the hack of the DNC, but all failed to note that my limited exchange with this alleged hacker through Twitter Direct Message only took place three months after WikiLeaks had already published the DNC and Clinton campaign material, and that the actual full text of our exchange was completely innocuous— providing no evidence whatsoever of either collusion or collaboration.

Mueller also concluded in his long-hidden report that he could find no evidence of the claim by right-wing gadfly Jerry Corsi that I had contacted Corsi in the wake of the shocking NBC disclosure that Donald Trump had joked about grabbing women by their genitalia and urged him to contact WikiLeaks publisher Julian Assange to urge Assange to expedite the release of the damaging material WikiLeaks had obtained regarding Hillary Clinton and the Democratic National Committee. Assange had alluded to in his public comments to this information for months. It was not a secret. Once again, this false narrative is repeatedly recycled despite its falsity.

The other "source" that is constantly pointed to as providing evidence of Russian collusion with the Trump campaign, as well as misdeeds on my part, is the "bipartisan" U.S. Senate Intelligence Committee Report pieced together by Senate Democrats with a band of Trump-hating establishment Republicans. I can report that every single reference to me in the report is factually incorrect and most of the allegations against me were simply cut and pasted from various fake news media reports. I shredded the U.S. Senate Intelligence Committee Report.

https://www.thegatewaypundit.com/2020/08/roger-stone-exclusive-senate-intelligence-committee-report-russian-collusion-recycled-bunk/

My family and I were subjected to the most vicious, partisan witch-hunt in U.S. history, in which we were virtually bankrupted and in which I faced a prison sentence of seven to nine years while having done absolutely nothing wrong—simply because I refused the government pressure to testify falsely against President Trump. It is only because of my faith in Jesus Christ that I have survived this ordeal. President Donald Trump recognized both the falsity of the charges against me and the entirely political motivation in my prosecution, commuting my prison sentence a mere forty-eight hours before I was to be remanded to a dank federal prison in Georgia, and subsequently issuing me a full and unconditional presidential pardon.

This latest attack on me using a completely fabricated and AI-generated audio attributing to me threats that I never made is only the latest attempt to smear and destroy me. This comes on the heels of false testimony before the January 6th Committee by former White House Aide Cassidy Hutchinson, who perjured herself when she claimed that, at President Trump's direction, White House Chief of Staff Mark Meadows called me and General Michael Flynn on January 5th to "find out what was going to happen on January 6th." In fact, neither General Flynn or I have ever communicated with Mark Meadows on that date or any other date.

Any claim or implication that I knew in advance about, condoned, or was involved in any illegal activity at the Capitol on January 6th is categorically false, and there is no witness, no phone call, text message, encrypted message, chat thread, or e-mail that would prove otherwise. Neither was I involved, in any way, in efforts by President Donald Trump's lawyers to delay the certification of the Electoral College in the U.S. Senate on January 6th. In fact, claims by MSNBC, CNN, and others that I participated in meetings regarding this effort in a "War Room" in the Willard Hotel are also entirely false. In fact, three individual sources confirmed for The Washington Post that I was not involved in the legal efforts to delay the certification of the Electoral College.

My many partisan critics in the Democrat Party and among the lying fake news media are extraordinarily bitter about the fact that I escaped the deadly snare carefully laid for me by Congressman Adam Schiff and his cohorts on the House Intelligence Committee, working closely with Robert Mueller's prosecutors. I now know for a certainty that the Mueller team shared my e-mails obtained with a search warrant with Schiff and company, in order for the House Democrats to fashion innocuous "gotcha" questions that subsequently allowed me to be charged with lying under oath, despite the innocuous content of the trick questions.

Having survived the efforts to destroy me in the Russian Collusion Hoax, and having no involvement or legal responsibility for any illegal action on January 6th, the very same fake news media outlets now seek to smear me utilizing AI-generated audios which simple forensic examination prove to be entirely fraudulent.

ANIL: *Special Counsel Hur cited President Biden's portrayal of himself as an "elderly man with a poor memory" as a factor in declining to prosecute. How do you interpret this reasoning, and what do you think it signifies about accountability and transparency in government?*

ROGER: It is vital to note that Special Counsel Robert Hur, who was appointed by Biden Attorney General Merrick Garland to investigate President Joe Biden's retention of classified and top secret documents from both his time as Vice President and U.S. Senator, concluded that Biden had willfully retained such documents in violation of the law. Also in his final report, Hur noted that during his questioning of Biden, that the President exhibited substantial memory loss, including the inability to remember exactly when he served as Vice President, as well as the inability to remember the date of the death of his son, Beau Biden. Although Biden would later publicly brizzle over the Special Counsel raising the question of Biden's son's death, it was later determined that it was Biden himself who raised his son's death, rather than Special Counsel Robert Hur. Incredibly, while conceding that Biden had violated the law in his retention of classified and top secret documents - a crime for which former President Donald Trump is currently being prosecuted - Hur also recommended that given Biden's deteriorating mental capacity, that Biden not be prosecuted. Hur profesized that no jury would find Biden guilty because of his diminished mental state! Can there be any more stark example of our two-tiered justice system? Former President Trump had, as President, the authority to retain classified and top secret documents, as well as the power to declassify any document simply by declaring it so. As Vice President, Joe Biden had no such authority or power. President Trump has also argued that the Presidential Records Act of 1978 gives him the full unilateral authority to decide what documents he can retain and what documents he will return to the National Archives.

ANIL: *The recent study examining potential voter fraud in the 2020 election, based on data from the Heartland Institute and Rasmussen Reports, has gained significant attention. Former President Trump has labeled this December survey as "the biggest story of the year," emphasizing the importance of addressing potential voter fraud in 2020 Elections. How do you see these findings impacting public trust in the electoral process, and what steps do you believe should be taken to address concerns raised by such studies?*

ROGER: Despite the very best efforts by the mainstream media to censor any information regarding irregularities, anomalies, and voter fraud in the 2020 election, as well as the naked attempt to delegitimize and silence anyone who has produced hard evidence of widespread voter fraud, it's amazing that a majority of Americans rightly suspect that the results of the 2020 election were corrupted.

Using the Covid-19 pandemic as an excuse, the Democrats and their allies buried within the bureaucracies of President Trump's own government moved systematically to change state election laws in the crucial swing states to allow for expanding early voting, mail-in ballots, and the establishment of drop boxes to receive ballots—all making widespread voter fraud much easier. Sadly, the Republican National Committee did nothing in the face of this obvious groundwork that was laid in order to hijack the 2020 election. It is also unfortunate that despite raising millions of dollars, the Republican National Committee has launched no effort in the crucial swing states to reform state election laws in order to curtail voter fraud. Given the successful effort by the Democrats and their allies in the dominant media to successfully perpetuate the hijacking of the 2020 election, I believe we can expect the same actors to engage in the exact same abuses in 2024. I believe the Trump campaign and the Republican National Committee have to be legally and technically prepared to identify, document, and legally challenge election fraud in real time in the 2024 election. I also believe that the Trump campaign must work tirelessly to maximize turnout of the President's supporters; in 2016, for example, 75% of evangelical Christians turned out to vote, while in 2020 that number dropped to 65%.

You can follow Roger Stone at StoneZONE.com

Brogue Signature By Capitol Times Media LLC

www.broguesignature.com

In 2018 Mr. Buddy Hall saw that President Donald J. Trump did not have a campaign tour bus so Buddy used his own funds and bought the Rolls Royce of tour buses, a Prevost H3-45 and had it professionally wrapped as the TRUMP TRAIN. Buddy toured the country promoting who he called the GREATEST President the USA has ever had, President Donald J. Trump. As millions of people witnessed, the TRUMP TRAIN led many Trump vehicle parades all over the USA

including the world record holder of the largest Trump vehicle parade ever with 41,000 (forty one thousand) vehicles which measured 91 miles long as registered by the Arizona Highway patrol. The TRUMP TRAIN also made may other appearances at many Boaters for Trump events, at the Trump Hotel in Las Vegas, at Mount Rushmore, Biker Trump parades at Sturgis with Bikers for Trump and a large event with My Pillow Mike Lindell and Diamond and Silk in Somerset Wisconsin. . Many famous Trump supporters have either been with the Trump Train or had the bus at their events such as President Trump, Donald Trump Jr, his fiancé Kimberly Guilfoyle, My Pillow owner Mike Lindell, Diamond and Silk, Arizona Congressman David Sweikhart, Arizona Congressman Paul Gosar, Kentucky Senator Rand Paul, Florida Congressman Matt Gaetz, Georgia Congress lady Marjorie Taylor Green, Arizona Sheriff Joe Apario, Arizona Sheriff Mark Lamb, Wisconsin Sheriff David Clark, National Radio host Wayne Allen Root, Former Trump attorney Sidney Powell, President Trumps personal photographer Gene Ho and family, Pastor Greg Locke, Dukes of Hazard star John Schneider, Roger Stone, Martha Boneta Fain, Patriot Street Fighter Scott McKay and too many more to list. Mr. Buddy Hall the owner of the former Trump Train sold the bus when the 2020 election was stolen and now that he sees how great President Trump is doing. People are asking Buddy to buy another Prevost H3-45 and get it wrapped as a new TRUMP TRAIN and get back on the road promoting President Trump again and leading many more Trump parades, Rallys and many other Trump events. Buddys funds are low since he used his money from the sale of the prior Trump Train bus to invest in real-estate and it is not selling due to high interest rates and for the first time he is asking for a few sponsors, and he will place the sponsors names or Logos etc in the new wrap design if it is a company or group and he also is asking for donations from private individuals to help make all of this happen again.

YOU CAN DONATE AT THE GIVE SEND GO

WEBSITE AT THE BOTTOM OF THE PAGE OR CALL OR TEXT MR. BUDDY HALL AT 228-222-1500 TO MAKE A DONATION OR TO BOOK THE TRUMP TRAIN TO COME TO YOUR CITY OR AN EVENT YOU MAY BE PLANNING.

Buddy Hall with Congresswoman Marjorie Taylor Green

Buddy Hall and Lana Hall with Roger Stone

Buddy Hall and Lana Hall with Kimberly Guilfoyle & Donald Trump Jr

Presidents Trumps photographer Gene HO

The Trump Train helps draw large crowds. If you agree with us and feel President Donald J. Trump deserves a 2024 Trump Train campaign tour bus, **PLEASE make a donation at http://www.givesendgo.com/thetrumptrain** and share this with many others on your social media and ask them to make a donation as well to give the GREATEST President EVER a campaign tour bus.

NOTICE: Once the Trump Train bus is finished touring the USA a year or so after President Trump is re-elected in 2024, the Trump Train bus will be put up for sale by a trusted 3rd party and ALL TOTAL GROSS proceeds will be bank wired by the buyer to a trusted 3rd party of President Trumps for them to donate to a few of President Trumps favorite charities. So not only will your donation or sponsorship help acquire a 2024 Trump Train tour bus now, but your donation or sponsorship will help President Trumps favorite charities in the near future.

DONATE AT www.givesendgo.com/thetrumptrain

Special Interview with

Mark Middleton

AMERICAN PATRIOT RELIEF

www.americanpatriotrelife.org

Anil: Today, we have the distinct pleasure of interviewing Mark and Jalise Middleton, from American Patriot Relief. Mark and Jalise are passionate advocates for our nation's heroes, embodying the spirit of patriotism and service in their work.

So, can you share more about your upbringing in Texas and how it influenced your values and lifestyle?

Mark: We both grew up in Arlington, Texas. We were not far from each other; we even had many of the same friends, but we did not meet one another until we were 14 years old. We both come from middle-class families and are the youngest in our families. She has two brothers; one has now passed away. I have one sister and four brothers. Jalise's father was a very noble man and a union steward in the aerospace industry. He took to the picket lines with three young children, and at another time, he planned a walk out at their oldest son's junior high school when there were ethical issues the school was unwilling to resolve. Jalise points to those hard moments of integrity and standing ground that have influenced her to this day. Other than that, our upbringing was typical for the 1970s and 80s. We drank from the water hose, had to be in when the streetlights came on, and got whooped for doing something wrong. We met at age 14 and began dating at age 16; we married at age 19.

Anil: What led to your decision to move to the country to care for your ailing father, and how did that experience shape your family dynamics?

Mark: The farm we live on is her family's land in far north Texas. In 2008, her father became very ill. She had always promised him that she would take care of him when he needed her and that she would never allow him to go to a nursing home.

The Lord had already called us to the farm, but we ran from the call instead of obeying, just years prior to her father's health failing. We really loved our home, neighborhood, and friends that we had in the city, but God had bigger plans. Living in the county was a welcome change for our family. While Texas is a conservative state, being in rural Texas was a breath of fresh air. Our kids adapted well. While financially difficult for a time, the slower pace was and still is a pleasant experience.

We were also able to hold to strong Christian, conservative values for our family with less influence from a steadily degrading society.

Anil: How did your faith play a role in your family life and community involvement over the years?

Mark: We both came to Christ in 1999. When we moved to the farm, we felt like we were in a spiritual desert. This sounds strange, given that most people in rural areas attend church regularly. We were used to a spiritually alive church with strong messages each week. This is not what we found. In 2020, we found our current church home. It is everything we want spiritually. Since our J6 experience, our church has rallied around us.

Our faith in Jesus Christ has been our rock over the last three years. I do not know how anyone could endure the weight of the federal government without the Spirit of God living in them.

We have been very involved in our community both in Arlington and in the country. God has called us to serve Him and others. We have devoted our lives to serving and volunteering wherever we are led.

Anil: Can you elaborate on Mark's journey from being a machinist to pursuing a master's degree in theology later in life?

Mark: Jalise's dad owned a small machine shop in Arlington and taught me to run and set up lathes and milling machines as well as read blueprints. From there, I got a job as a maintenance machinist, There I learned how to TiG weld. later learned CNC programing and industrial robotics. From early on in our Christian walk I felt God prompting me to teach, in 2010 I preached an Easter message in a horse pasture. That group I preached to asked if I would pastor a new church they wanted to start. I accepted the offer. During this I was growing tired of working in the industrial settings and wanted to move on. In 2011 I started school to finish my BS in business management. once I earned that degree, I felt God's prompting to pursue my master's in theology. I no long felt the desire to pastor, but rather to teach His Word.

Anil: What were your initial thoughts and emotions when the FBI conducted the raid on your home in April 2021?

Mark: Honestly, we thought it was a joke. Not like a prank, but rather the DOJ just wanting to scare and embarrass us and to intimidate others from speaking out. We thought they would eventually drop all charges like they had been doing for BLM and Antifa protesters. After all, our involvement on that day was nothing like the riots of 2020.

Anil: How did the false portrayal of you in the media and the subsequent loss of your jobs impact you and your family?

Mark: The impact was deep and harsh. We immediately lost our jobs. It seemed that everyone we knew abandoned us, as if we had a scarlet letter placed on us. The liberal media hounded us and our children. People, even family avoided us. It was next to impossible to get a job are remain at one for more than a few weeks. The liberal mob would Dox us and bombard our new employer with negative calls and social media post. Our social media accounts had been shut down; cell phones confiscated. A community that knew our integrity and character for many years now believed the lies of strangers in the media.

Anil: What steps have you taken to defend yourselves against the federal charges you're facing, considering you maintain your innocence?

Mark: Originally, we had private attorneys. The cost to defend ourselves was $250,000. About 1 ½ years into the battle we had paid out $70,000 for legal fees. At this point we realized we were going to be bankrupt by trying to keep our attorneys. We tried to take a lien against our 4-generation owned family land.

We believed the government was interfering with that process also. The Lord spoke to Jalise in a dream by showing her that the same God that provided the finances to pay for the hired attorneys was the same God that could work through a public defender. So we fired our attorneys and went with Public Defenders. Our mind set was we can go to jail bankrupt with private attorneys, or we can just go to jail. Our trial started on 2/5/2024. It lasted 7 days. We were convicted on all charges.

Anil: Could you explain the motivation behind founding the nonprofit organization American Patriot Relief and the services it provides to January 6th defendants and their families?

Mark: God called us to serve Him and serve people. After our arrest, we spent about 2 months in isolation at home praying and reading scripture. During that time God called us to **"be His hand and feet"** We personally were in a better position in life than most J6ers because just a year earlier He compelled us to become debt free. Everything paid off, children are grown and independent. So, it made since that we should be the ones to do this. When a friend of ours faced a very similar situation, being raided by the FBI, we went to minister to him. Through that encounter with Terry Anderson, the three of us formed American Patriot Relief.

American Patriot Relief has pulled homes out of foreclosure, housed homeless J6ers defendants, repaired cars, flown families to see their hostage, Paid travel expenses for J6 defendants and their families to get to trial and sentencing. We provide commissary through an "Adopt-a-J6er" program that allows the public to search through photos to pick the hostage the Lord leads them to support, and we load their donation directly on to their commissary funds each month as a hassle-free way to support the J6 community.

We provide a hotline service to help with the emotional trauma that comes from this political assault, while providing resources to help them with their physical needs. We also have a commissary general fund where people can donate to www.j6commissaryfund.org. We provide a freedom nest program where patriots across the country volunteer their homes to allow overnight stays and a hot meal at no charge to January 6 defendants while they travel. We also host prayer vigils each Tuesday at 6 pm central time by zoom where we connect into Freedom Corner to show support for the DC Gulag hostages, and Micki Witthoeft (Ashli Babbitt's mother). We also host a Monday night zoom mixer to get to know the board that is open to the public to bring questions, concerns and to brainstorm. Lastly, We provide J6 defendants for public speaking engagements to educate the public on the atrocities happening right here on our soil.

Anil: How has the support from American Patriot Relief and the broader community affected your outlook and determination in facing the legal challenges ahead?

Mark: APR was founded in August of 2022. We formed a board of like-minded patriots that not only helped build APR, but also helped us emotionally deal with our circumstances. We quickly gained a following on social media and good working relationship with other J6 support organizations.

Being as involved as we are, we heard all the horror stories of the other J6ers. Not only the legal woes, but also the financial and emotional struggles. Through all of this it has been oddly therapeutic, Working with APR and focusing on the needs of others over our own needs kept us humble, with a servant heart. It helped us walk through our pain and focus on the mission instead of ourselves. It gave us a platform to speak Jesus to the world at a time in our nation's history where it is most critical. Serving in this way gave us a front row seat to the love and faithfulness of Jesus Christ for His people. This has been the greatest honor of our lives to serve Jesus, and the J6community in this way. We see that we are trodding in Christs foot steps...You know? Jesus was accused of insurrection too!!! What an honor that He trusts us to be obedient and faithful for such a high calling.

Anil: Looking ahead, what are your hopes and goals for the future, both personally and for the organization you've established?

Mark: For APR, Our motto is "J6 and beyond", Even if/when we solve the J6 sham, there will always be government overreach and persecution of innocents. Our goal is to continue to meet those needs as well as work to promote ethical government both federal and state. We will continue to serve Jesus and His persecuted followers, along with those that stand for what is right and others attempt to destroy them for the noble act.

For us personally, We plan to full time RV along the gulf coast, spend time with our 6 grandkids and travel to events all around the county educating people about J6 and other legal/political issues and raise money for APR. We plan to become inspirational public speakers and maybe even author a devotional noting our walk through the pain, and God's faithfulness.

CAPITOL TIMES MAGAZINE
GET YOUR
SUBSCRIPTION
TODAY
www.capitoltimesmagazine/magazine-subscription

By David Colbert

HILLARY CLINTON'S

DISCONNECT WITH AMERICAN VOTERS: A LESSON IN POLITICAL HUBRIS

Hillary Clinton, the perennial figure in American politics, has once again found herself entangled in controversy, this time for her dismissive and condescending remarks towards voters who dare to question the Biden administration's policies. Her recent appearance on The Tonight Show with Jimmy Fallon revealed a startling disconnect with the concerns and frustrations of everyday Americans, underscoring why her political advice often falls on deaf ears.

During her interview, when asked about voters' reluctance to support President Joe Biden due to pressing issues such as the border crisis, inflation, and the push for electric vehicle mandates, Clinton's response was nothing short of contemptuous. "Get over yourself," she sneered, summarily dismissing the legitimate concerns of millions of Americans as inconsequential.

Moreover, Clinton attempted to justify her stance by invoking former President Donald Trump's legal woes, claiming that voters had no choice in the matter due to Trump facing "91 criminal charges." This desperate deflection not only reeks of political opportunism but also underscores a fundamental misunderstanding of the electorate's motivations and priorities.

In a surprising turn of events, ESPN's Stephen A. Smith openly criticized Clinton's patronizing attitude towards voters, labeling her remarks as "silly" and emblematic of why she faced defeat in the 2016 election. Smith astutely pointed out that Clinton's reliance on tired slogans and divisive rhetoric, such as labeling Trump's presidency as "not normal," failed to resonate with voters then and continues to ring hollow now. Indeed, Clinton's failure to internalize the lessons from her past electoral losses highlights a troubling pattern of political hubris. By dismissing valid concerns and resorting to partisan attacks, she alienates the very voters whose support she desperately needs to remain relevant in today's political landscape.

The essence of democracy lies in respecting differing viewpoints and engaging in constructive dialogue, not in denigrating dissenting voices with arrogance and disdain. Clinton's insistence on perpetuating a narrative of moral superiority only serves to widen the ideological chasm that divides our nation.

As conservatives, we believe in the power of genuine empathy and inclusive leadership. It is incumbent upon political figures like Hillary Clinton to listen to the concerns of all Americans, regardless of their political leanings, and to offer solutions grounded in pragmatism, not partisanship.

Smith's critique is a sobering reminder of the dangers of political elitism and detachment from the realities faced by ordinary voters. Clinton's fixation on portraying Trump as "abnormal" and unfit for office failed to resonate with working-class Americans who were grappling with economic anxieties and disillusionment with the political establishment.

Moreover, Smith's analysis extends beyond Clinton's failed campaign tactics to highlight broader shortcomings within the Democratic Party's current approach. He warns against the dangers of repeating past mistakes, cautioning against a campaign strategy that prioritizes fear-mongering and divisive rhetoric over substantive policy solutions.

Indeed, the parallels between Clinton's ill-fated 2016 campaign and President Joe Biden's current reelection bid are striking. Biden, much like Clinton, has resorted to baseless attacks on Trump's character and integrity, falsely painting him as a threat to democracy. This recycled strategy not only reeks of desperation but also underscores a fundamental disconnect with the priorities and concerns of the American electorate.

In contrast, Trump's reelection campaign is resonating with voters precisely because it speaks directly to their lived experiences and challenges. By prioritizing issues such as border security, economic stability, and ending foreign entanglements like the war in Ukraine, Trump is tapping into the grassroots concerns of "forgotten" Americans who feel marginalized by the political elite.

Recent polling data corroborates this sentiment, showing Trump in a stronger position than ever before. His unwavering commitment to prioritizing the needs of working-class Americans is a stark contrast to Biden's hollow promises and divisive fear-mongering.

As an American, we applaud Trump's authentic engagement with the American people and reject the cynical tactics employed by Biden and Clinton. The path to electoral success lies not in denigrating political opponents but in offering genuine solutions to the pressing challenges facing our nation.

Hillary Clinton's misguided campaign tactics serve as a cautionary tale for the Biden administration and the broader Democratic Party. By prioritizing fear over substance and elitism over empathy, they risk repeating the mistakes of the past and alienating the very voters they seek to represent. It is time to pivot towards a politics of inclusivity and authenticity, one that truly puts the interests of the American people first.

Advertisment

Brogue Signature by Capitol Times Media LLC

www.broguesignature.com

BROGUE
Signature

LET'S
PLAY
With Color

BeYOUtifu

www.broguesignature.com

THE HUNTER BIDEN SAGA:

Questionable Meetings and Congressional Defiance

By Mary Jones

The latest developments surrounding Hunter Biden's legal battles and his defiance of a congressional subpoena have once again brought the spotlight on the Biden family's entanglements and raised troubling questions about the transparency and integrity of the White House.

Recent revelations indicate that Abbe Lowell, Hunter Biden's attorney, held a meeting with Anthony Bernal, a top aide to first lady Jill Biden, in the East Wing of the White House just days before Hunter Biden chose to disregard a congressional subpoena. The timing of this meeting raises eyebrows, particularly given the subsequent actions of Hunter Biden and the implications for the ongoing congressional investigation.

Hunter Biden's decision to snub the House Oversight and Accountability Committee's subpoena and instead stage a press conference at the Capitol Senate side underscores a pattern of defiance and evasion. Rather than cooperating with legitimate inquiries, Hunter Biden opted to dismiss the investigation as "illegitimate" and absolve his father of any involvement in his questionable business dealings abroad.

Moreover, White House press secretary Karine Jean-Pierre's acknowledgment that President Joe Biden was "familiar" with his son's intentions on the day of the subpoena defiance raises further concerns about potential interference or influence exerted from the highest levels of government.

The meeting between Lowell and Bernal, coinciding with a White House Hanukkah reception, adds a layer of complexity to this narrative. While the White House has downplayed the significance of this encounter, questions linger about the nature and scope of discussions held behind closed doors, particularly in light of Hunter Biden's subsequent actions.

The credibility of Hunter Biden's claims regarding his father's purported lack of involvement in his business ventures remains dubious, given the mounting evidence to the contrary. Allegations of financial entanglements with foreign entities, including Burisma in Ukraine and Chinese private businessmen, continue to cast a shadow over the Biden family's ethical conduct and raise legitimate concerns about potential conflicts of interest.

As conservatives, we demand transparency and accountability from our elected officials and their families. The apparent collusion between Hunter Biden's legal representative and the first lady's top aide, coupled with Hunter's blatant disregard for congressional oversight, underscores the urgent need for a thorough and impartial investigation into the Biden family's activities.

It is imperative that Congress exercises its constitutional duty to uphold the rule of law and ensure that no individual, regardless of political affiliation, is above accountability. The American people deserve clarity and integrity in their government, free from the shadow of corruption and undue influence.

In conclusion, the unfolding saga of Hunter Biden's legal woes and the Biden family's dubious associations demands a sober examination of ethical standards and adherence to constitutional principles. As conservatives, we remain steadfast in our commitment to upholding the principles of transparency, accountability, and integrity in government, regardless of political consequences.

BROGUE

Signature

Discover Your Style

www.broguesignature.com

The Unfolding Electoral Landscape:

A Christian Conservative Perspective

By Sunil Anwar

Recent polling data from USA TODAY/Suffolk University paints a concerning picture for President Joe Biden's reelection prospects, showcasing a neck-and-neck race with former President Donald Trump and highlighting significant challenges facing the Biden administration. In a volatile electorate, former President Trump edges out President Biden by a narrow margin, with Trump garnering 40% support compared to Biden's 38%.

This statistical tie underscores the unsettled sentiment prevailing among voters, with one in four indicating they might change their minds before November. Notably, a substantial portion of both Biden and Trump supporters remains open to reconsidering their choices, reflecting the fluidity of the current political landscape.

As Christian conservatives, we are deeply concerned about the direction our nation is headed, particularly under the leadership of President Biden. The findings of these polls mirror the sentiments of many Americans who are troubled by the current state of affairs and are seeking leadership that aligns with their values and concerns.

The poll's revelation that immigration and challenges to democracy are top concerns for voters is significant. Immigration is not merely an economic or political issue; it is a moral and ethical concern deeply rooted in our Christian values. We believe in respecting the rule of law and upholding the sovereignty of our borders while demonstrating compassion towards those seeking refuge.

Furthermore, the erosion of trust in our democratic institutions is alarming. As Christian conservatives, we cherish the principles of liberty and justice for all, and any threat to our democratic norms is a cause for serious reflection and action.

The issue of abortion, which resonates strongly with Christian conservatives, rightfully holds a prominent place in the minds of voters. President Biden's administration has been disappointingly pro-abortion, undermining the sanctity of human life and disregarding the values cherished by millions of Americans.

Additionally, a recent ABC/Ipsos poll highlights Biden's deficit against Trump on key issues. Trump enjoys higher levels of trust across a range of policy areas, underscoring a growing perception of Biden's inadequacies in addressing critical national concerns. Notably, Trump outpaces Biden on issues related to the economy, national security, and immigration, further complicating Biden's reelection prospects.

The palpable erosion of public trust in President Biden's leadership underscores broader dissatisfaction with his administration's performance. Despite campaign promises and ambitious policy agendas, Biden has struggled to allay fundamental concerns about economic stability, national security, and immigration enforcement. As the election approaches, Biden faces a formidable task of reconnecting with disillusioned voters and conveying a compelling vision for America's future.

The electorate's receptiveness to Trump's message underscores a yearning for decisive leadership and tangible solutions to pressing challenges. Biden must pivot decisively, demonstrating resolve and addressing legitimate concerns to regain lost ground and secure a path to victory.

As we navigate this pivotal election season, Christian conservatives must remain steadfast in our convictions and values.

We cannot afford to compromise on issues that are fundamental to our faith and our nation's well-being. It is incumbent upon us to support leaders who uphold the sanctity of life, defend our borders, protect religious freedom, and preserve the foundational principles that have made America a beacon of hope and opportunity.

In conclusion, the shifting dynamics of the upcoming election demand thoughtful consideration and decisive action from Christian conservatives. Let us unite in prayer and purpose, seeking leaders who will honor God and advance policies that reflect our deeply held beliefs. Together, we can steer our nation towards a brighter future rooted in faith, freedom, and moral integrity.

Advertsiement

Subscribe today to gain exclusive access to in-depth analysis, thought-provoking commentary, and expert opinions. Stay informed and engaged with the latest developments shaping our nation and world.

Subscribe now to Capitol Times Magazine and elevate your understanding of conservative principles and ideologies.

SUBSCRIBE TODAY AND GET STARTED!

www.capitoltimesmedia.com/magazine-subscription

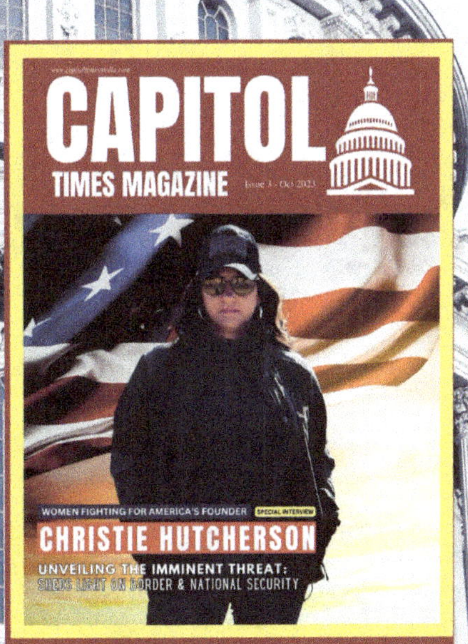

Capitol Times Magazine
RELIGION SECTION

Matthew 21:22 - And whatever you ask in prayer, you will receive, if you have faith.

CHRISTIAN PERSECUTION IN ISLAMIC COUNTRIES:
A Call for Action and Support

By Pastor AS John

Christian persecution in Islamic countries, such as Pakistan and other nations, is a deeply concerning issue that demands global attention and concerted efforts to protect religious freedoms and human rights. The systematic discrimination, violence, and oppression faced by Christians in these regions underscore the urgent need for international intervention, including support from the United States of America.

Understanding the Situation

In many Islamic countries, Christians are a minority population subjected to various forms of persecution:

Discrimination and Marginalization: Christians often face discrimination in employment, education, and social services, limiting their opportunities and quality of life.

Violence and Attacks: Extremist groups target Christian communities through acts of violence, including bombings, shootings, and mob attacks on churches and individuals.

Blasphemy Laws: Stringent blasphemy laws are used to unfairly target and imprison Christians based on false accusations of insulting Islam.

Forced Conversions: Christian girls and women are particularly vulnerable to abduction, forced marriage to Muslim men, and conversion to Islam against their will.

Solutions and U.S. Involvement

To address Christian persecution in Islamic countries, the United States can take proactive steps:

1. **Diplomatic Pressure:** The U.S. government should use diplomatic channels to urge Islamic countries to uphold religious freedom and protect minority rights.
2. **Humanitarian Aid and Assistance:** Provide financial support and resources to organizations working to aid persecuted Christians, including refugee assistance and legal aid.
3. **Advocacy and Awareness:** Raise awareness about religious persecution through international forums, media campaigns, and diplomatic engagements to mobilize global support.
4. **Policy Review and Sanctions:** Evaluate foreign aid and trade agreements with countries that systematically violate religious freedoms, imposing sanctions or conditions for improvement.

The Role of Civil Society and International Organizations
• **Faith-Based Organizations:** Collaborate with religious and humanitarian groups to provide support, advocacy, and relief efforts for persecuted Christians.
• **United Nations:** Encourage the United Nations and other international bodies to prioritize religious freedom and address human rights violations against minorities.

Christian persecution in Islamic countries demands immediate attention and action from the global community, including the United States. It is imperative to stand in solidarity with persecuted Christians, advocate for their rights, and hold oppressive regimes accountable for their actions. By leveraging diplomatic, humanitarian, and advocacy efforts, we can work towards a world where all individuals can practice their faith freely and without fear of persecution.

The United States, with its commitment to democracy and human rights, has a vital role to play in promoting religious freedom and defending persecuted Christians worldwide. Together, through collective action and unwavering determination, we can make a meaningful difference in the lives of those suffering due to their religious beliefs.

SUMMER FASHION

INSPIRATION DAILY WEAR

Inspire Your Fashion Choices Every Day, Creating Unique and Stunning Styles.

www.broguesignature.com

Studiodragonfly 19®

Capitol Times Magazine
Business Section

HOW TO START A CONSERVATIVE BUSINESS:

A Practical Guide

By James Anderson

Starting a conservative business in the United States requires careful planning, strategic decision-making, and a clear understanding of market dynamics. Whether you're looking to launch a new venture or align an existing business with conservative values, here's a detailed guide to help you navigate the process successfully:

1. Define Your Niche and Market

- Identify Your Conservative Audience: Determine the specific segment of the conservative market you want to target. This could include sectors such as traditional values, pro-life advocacy, Second Amendment rights, free-market entrepreneurship, or patriotic merchandise.

- Research Market Demand: Conduct thorough market research to assess the demand for conservative products or services in your chosen niche. Look for gaps in the market that your business can fill effectively.

2. Develop a Solid Business Plan

- Set Clear Goals: Define your business objectives, target market, unique selling proposition (USP), and revenue projections.

- Outline Financials: Detail your startup costs, funding sources, pricing strategy, and financial forecasts for the first few years of operation.

- Legal Structure: Choose an appropriate legal structure for your business (e.g., LLC, corporation, sole proprietorship) and register your business with the relevant authorities.

3. Establish Your Brand Identity

- Craft a Strong Brand Message: Define your brand's values, mission statement, and messaging to resonate with conservative consumers.

- Design a Compelling Brand Image: Create a professional logo, website, and marketing materials that reflect conservative values and appeal to your target audience.

4. Navigate Regulatory and Compliance Requirements

• Understand Legal Obligations: Familiarize yourself with federal, state, and local regulations that apply to your industry and business operations.

• Obtain Necessary Licenses and Permits: Secure any required licenses, permits, or certifications to operate your business legally.

5. Build Strategic Partnerships and Networks

• Engage with Conservative Organizations: Network with conservative groups, think tanks, and associations to build partnerships and gain support for your business.

• Collaborate with Like-Minded Businesses: Form alliances with other conservative businesses or influencers to amplify your reach and credibility.

6. Develop and Market Your Products or Services

- Offer Value-Driven Products/Services: Develop high-quality offerings that align with conservative values and address the needs of your target market.

- Implement Effective Marketing Strategies: Utilize conservative media outlets, social media platforms, and grassroots campaigns to promote your business and connect with potential customers.

7. Embrace Conservative Principles in Operations

- Prioritize Ethical Practices: Adhere to conservative principles of honesty, integrity, and transparency in all business dealings.
- Support American-Made Products: Whenever possible, source products and materials from U.S.-based suppliers to support domestic manufacturing and local economies.

8. Stay Informed and Adapt

- Monitor Political and Economic Trends: Stay abreast of legislative changes, policy developments, and market shifts that may impact your business.
- Adapt to Changing Landscapes: Be flexible and willing to adapt your business strategies to meet evolving consumer preferences and industry trends.

Starting a conservative business in the United States requires resilience, dedication, and a commitment to conservative values. By following these steps and staying true to your principles, you can build a successful business that resonates with like-minded consumers and contributes positively to the conservative movement.

RISING HOUSING COSTS DIMINISH HOMEOWNERSHIP DREAMS

By Mary Jones

A recent survey commissioned by Redfin and conducted by Qualtrics has shed light on the growing concerns among renters in the United States about their ability to achieve homeownership amidst soaring housing costs and mortgage rates.

According to the survey, which involved 3,000 respondents including 1,000 renters, a staggering 38 percent of renters expressed doubts about ever being able to own a home. This figure marks a significant increase from 27 percent in 2023, underscoring the mounting challenges faced by aspiring homeowners.

The primary reason cited for this disillusionment is the lack of affordability in the housing market. With home prices skyrocketing and mortgage rates climbing, many renters feel increasingly disconnected from the American dream of owning a home.

according to Breitbart News, Redfin's Chief Economist, Daryl Fairweather, highlighted the stark realities driving this trend. "Housing costs are high across the board," Fairweather remarked, "but renting is a more affordable and realistic option for many Americans right now—especially those who have never owned a home and aren't able to tap into equity from a previous sale."

The survey findings underscore a broader economic concern: the widening gap between housing affordability and the financial capacity of aspiring homeowners. As homeownership becomes increasingly elusive for many, the implications extend beyond personal aspirations to impact broader economic indicators and societal dynamics.

Biden's Immigration Policies Fuel Housing Affordability Crisis

The studies highlighting the struggles of young Americans to afford housing and save for the future underscore a troubling reality exacerbated by President Joe Biden's immigration policies. As housing costs soar and homelessness rises, it's clear that Biden's open border approach is contributing to a worsening affordability crisis across the nation.

The St. Louis Federal Reserve's Institute for Economic Equity found that one in three individuals from Generation Z faces income challenges and holds a pessimistic view of the economy.

This demographic group, crucial for future economic growth, is increasingly unable to achieve basic financial milestones like homeownership and retirement savings.

Similarly, data from the Joint Center for Housing Studies of Harvard University reveal the dire situation faced by renters, with a record number paying exorbitant portions of their income towards rent and utilities. The burden of housing costs is pushing many Americans towards financial strain and instability.

President Biden's lax immigration policies have played a significant role in exacerbating this crisis. Since taking office, nearly eight million migrants, including both legal and illegal immigrants, have entered the United States. The Congressional Budget Office estimates that over six million illegal migrants alone have entered the country under Biden's tenure.

The influx of migrants has driven population growth, intensifying demand for housing and leading to rising prices. The resultant shortage of affordable housing has contributed to a troubling surge in homelessness, with an 11 percent increase observed between 2022 and 2023, as reported by the Wall Street Journal.

Biden's failure to secure the southern border and manage immigration responsibly has imposed substantial economic costs on American citizens, particularly the most vulnerable segments of society. The strain on housing affordability, coupled with broader economic challenges, highlights the urgent need for a reevaluation of immigration policies that prioritize the interests and well-being of American citizens.

As we confront the housing affordability crisis and its social ramifications, it is imperative that policymakers address the root causes, including the impact of unsustainable immigration policies. The future prosperity of our nation hinges on policies that promote economic opportunity, safeguard American workers, and preserve the fundamental values of homeownership and financial security.

BROGUE SIGNATURE

CHAMPION T-SHIRT SUSTAINABLE FASHION, UNPARALLELED STYLE

KENNEDY INTERNATIONAL LOGISTICS & SERVICES, LLC

Kennedy International Logistics & Services (KILS) stands at the vanguard of global trade and safety, providing robust solutions in logistics, security, and ancillary services to clients who demand excellence. Founded on the principles of integrity, reliability, and service supremacy, KILSS is not just a company – it is a titan in safeguarding client interests across borders and through the toughest terrains. At KILSS, we understand that the world does not stand still, and neither do we.

Our ironclad commitment to facilitating seamless transactions and securing client operations has propelled us to the forefront of the industry. Armed with a fleet of advanced logistical assets, a global network that spans continents, and a dedicated team of experts who embody our mission, we deliver nothing short of invincible service. Our logistical services are engineered to meet the highest standards of timeliness and efficiency, ensuring that cargo reaches its destination with unyielding precision. From intricate supply chain solutions to expeditious freight forwarding, we move mountains, so your business doesn't have to. Security is not just an offering; it is etched into our framework.

KILS implements cutting-edge surveillance and protection protocols to safeguard your assets and operations. Our security personnel, drawn from the elite ranks of military and law enforcement, work tirelessly to provide a bulwark of defense in an unpredictable world. Beyond the core of logistics and security, KILSS amplifies its portfolio with a suite of services tailored to the unique needs of each client. Consultancy, risk assessment, and bespoke project implementations are but a few of the strategies we enact to ensure that your enterprise thrives in any environment.

The calling of Kennedy International Logistics & Services is clear: We are the iron shield and steadfast partner in your quest for business dominance. With KILS, your ambitions are unbounded, your assets unassailable, and your path to success carved in stone. We are the paragon of power and poise in an ever-changing global landscape - relentlessly moving forward, so you lead with confidence.

Why Kennedy International

Over-watch
Security
Close Protection
Armed security
assest protection
surveillance
border security
secure logistics

Contact:

Laurence Kennedy, CEO/Founder
Email:
contact@kennedyint.com
Office: (001) 800 322 3172
www.kennedyint.com

"""Real security can only be achieved via knowledge, experience, and ability"""
Laurence R. Kennedy, CEO/Founder

Subscribe today to gain exclusive access to in-depth analysis, thought-provoking commentary, and expert opinions. Stay informed and engaged with the latest developments shaping our nation and world.

Subscribe now to Capitol Times Magazine and elevate your understanding of conservative principles and ideologies.

SUBSCRIBE TODAY AND GET STARTED!

www.capitoltimesmedia.com/magazine-subscription

PRAYER FOR
ISRAEL
WHOEVER BLESSES ISRAEL WILL BE BLESSED,
AND WHOEVER CURSES ISRAEL WILL BE CURSED."
NUMBERS 24:9

www.ingramcontent.com/pod-product-compliance
Lightning Source LLC
Chambersburg PA
CBHW081953160726
47999CB00008B/2610